MW01256512

LIVING THE TRUTH

JOSEF PIEPER

Living the Truth

The Truth of All Things
and
Reality and the Good

IGNATIUS PRESS   SAN FRANCISCO

Titles of the German originals:

Wahrheit der Dinge
© 1966 by Kösel Verlag, GmbH & Co.
Munich

Die Wirklichkeit und das Gute
© 1963 by Kösel Verlag GmbH & Co.
Munich

Cover design by Roxanne Mei Lum

ISBN 978-0-89870-261-3
ISBN 0-89870-261-5
Library of Congress Control Number 89-84891
Printed in the United States of America ∞

CONTENTS

The Truth of All Things

6 CONTENTS

6

Reality and the Good

The Truth of All Things

*An Inquiry into the Anthropology
of the High Middle Ages*

Translated
by
Lothar Krauth

INTRODUCTION

With the expression, "All that exists is true", Western philosophy for almost two millenia intended to make a statement not only about reality as such but no less about the nature of man. The great teachers of the High Middle Ages had uncritically absorbed the quintessence of Western traditional thought since earliest Greek times and thus represented it undistorted. These teachers above all took the seemingly "unrealistic" principle of the truth of all reality in fact as an anthropological statement that explained something about human nature. To show this is the first purpose of our study.

We do not set out, therefore, to defend the statement about the "truth of all things" with objective arguments, much less to "prove" it (a quite impossible task, after all). No, the intention is entirely to concentrate on interpretation alone. We wish to show the meaning of this statement within the ontology of the High Middle Ages. Consequently, we shall have to deal primarily with Thomas Aquinas, the outstanding representative of classical medieval metaphysics. It seems that in his thought there converged, for a brief historical moment, those lines that previously had searched, separately, for a focal point, and that soon afterward again diverged in different directions.

And yet, the ultimate purpose of our study does not concern history. Rather, through an exposition as meticulous and comprehensive as possible, we aim to draw out the far-reaching ontological dynamics inherent in this principle of the truth of all things.

"Yet the truth that dwells in the core of all things none but the few do contemplate."

Anselm of Canterbury
(*De veritate*, chap. 9)

Chapter One

I

Omne ens est verum,[1] all that is real, is true. Confronted with the concise sweep of this statement, we of these latter days are prone to feel intuitively an admiration for such grand simplicity, yet coupled with confusion, even with utter puzzlement as to the exact and specific meaning of those few words.

The other statement, *omne ens est bonum,* all that is, is good, equally a principle of classical Western metaphysics,[2] does not appear, if only on the surface, to be so totally inaccessible to our understanding. We of the post-Kantian era may at least think we understand it somehow, perhaps by identifying it with a certain thesis of liberalism (the mother of the notion that "man is essentially good"). But, of course, such an interpretation misses entirely the precise and original meaning of that principle. And the deceptive certainty of such an erroneous approach may well be more detrimental than the utter perplexity caused by the statement, "all that is real, is true".

Such, then, is indeed the situation: drawing only on prevailing and common thinking, the attempt to unlock the meaning of this statement will not succeed, not even in opening up a dead end.

Post-Kantian philosophy, here understood in a nonchronological sense, is of no help in this matter. All the textbooks, even those that lately claim again the occasional title of "ontology", omit any reference to the principle of the truth of all things.

---

[1] This expression, as far as I know, was not yet used by the Scholastics of the High Middle Ages. They consistently used *ens et verum convertuntur;* "to be" and "to be true" are equivalent. Thomas Aquinas *Ver.* 1, 10 formulates, *omnis res est vera et nulla res est falsa.*

[2] *Ver.* 21, 2; *ST* 1, 5, 3. Cf. Lotz, *Sein und Wert.*

LIVING THE TRUTH

2

In one of the Platonic Dialogues we find the statement, "what
is most noble (*ariston*) in all existing things, is truth."[3] Yet
Plato himself should not be seen as having originated the principle of the truth of all things. Not only Parmenides seems to
have known it, but Pythagoras as well;[4] and Pythagoras in
turn drew on a much more ancient tradition. Plato, however,
has given this concept its definitive expression for many centuries to come. He recognized and confirmed it as belonging
to the inalienable cultural patrimony of mankind. This is all
the more remarkable in view of what happened in the first major break in the Western philosophical tradition: Renaissance
humanism on the one hand despised and eliminated the principle of ontological truth, together with metaphysical ontology as such—while on the other hand drawing its own tenets,
especially its antitraditional stance, from the very same Platonic (or Neoplatonic) heritage. The same has to be said of the
reemerging Aristotelianism of that era. This new Aristotelianism had sprung mainly from Averroism and thus from
Neoplatonism;[5] it, too, attacked the Aristotelianism of the traditional Scholastics. Quite heterogeneous positions united in
the battle cry of that period: "No to Scholastic Aristotelianism!" *Dialectical Disputations against the Aristotelians:* this title
of a philosophical treatise by Lorenzo Valla stands for an entire
literary genus of that period. These *Disputations*, in a manner

---

[3] *Republic* 7, 532C.
[4] The Syrian philosopher Iamblichus (ca. 270–330), in his *De vita Pythago-
rica*, chap. 29, uses this expression: ἡ ἐν τοῖς οὖσιν ἀλήθεια. Willmann, who
excelled in researching the Pythagorean teachings, characterizes the "transcendentals" as "a group of concepts derived from combining the
Pythagorean principles of *unity* and *truth* with the Platonic principles of *being*
and *goodness*". Willmann, *Idealismus* 3:1036.
[5] Cf. Max Wundt, *Schulmetaphysik*, 38. It is also noteworthy that the *Theology of Aristotle*, excerpts from Plotinus' *Enneads* compiled in Arabic by a Syrian Christian in the ninth century, was printed 1519 in Rome (and again 1572
in Paris) with the title *Sapientissimi philosophi Aristotelis Stagiritae theologia sive
mystica philosophia secundum Aegyptios*. Cf. Überweg, *Geschichte*, 2:302f.

more passionate and rhetorical than profound, dismiss also the traditional teaching on "transcendentals",[6] the doctrine of those notions that "transcend" and encompass the different types and categories of all existing beings: the concepts of unity, truth and goodness.

The Renaissance humanists, then, are among the first to reject the principle of the truth of all things; they even deny that it expresses anything meaningful at all.

The stagnating and sterile conceptual framework of late Scholasticism no doubt needed to be shaken up drastically. But for almost a century the "protest" against every traditional notion knew no bounds; in Goethe's words, "not least and especially in all branches of science". So much so that "Francis Bacon finally had the audacity to wipe out everything written so far on the slate of humanity." Goethe notes "insensitivity of *Bacon* toward the values of antiquity" and calls it "very unpleasant". For "who can listen impassively when Bacon compares the works of Aristotle and Plato to lightweight planks that are easily washed up on our shores by the streams of time, precisely because they lack robust and meaningful substance."[7] It should come as no surprise, therefore, that Bacon erases the concept of transcendentals not only from "science" but from metaphysics as well. Incidentally, he dismisses them in such a haughty and summary way that he even fails to mention at all the concept of transcendental truth, that is to say, the concept of the truth of all things.[8]

---

[6] Thomas Aquinas' teaching on these concepts is explained in chapter 2, section 2. The term *transcendentia* or *transcendentalia* apparently originated with Albertus Magnus; cf. Knittermeyer, *Terminus*, 17, where Albertus is quoted mentioning a reality *quod genera transcendit, ut est res, unum et aliquid* (*Liber de Praedicabilibus* 4, 3). Thomas Aquinas, in *De natura generis* (not unanimously accepted as authentic, but so considered, e.g., by Grabmann), chap. 2, explicitly mentions the *sex transcendentia*.

[7] Goethe, *Farbenlehre*, 572–76.

[8] Bacon, *Works* 3:4.

3

We shall briefly consult some other thinkers who, like Bacon, should be counted among the ancestors and founding fathers of "modern" philosophy and science.

Bacon's compatriot *Hobbes* is quite familiar with the principle of ontological truth. But for him this concept of the "metaphysicians" is "inane and childish".[9] *Veritas enim in dicto, non in re consistit*: there is no truth in things.[10]

Descartes explicitly decides to get away from all philosophical tradition, and this should not be overlooked[11] in spite of ample evidence that he, too, is influenced by it. True, he still writes *Meditationes de prima philosophia*, that is, meditations on metaphysics; and the fourth of these meditations is entitled "On Truth and Falsehood". Yet not a word is found in it about the truth of all things. "For Descartes, there is no truth in things."[12]

Spinoza, in his *Cogitata metaphysica*, mentions the concept of the truth of all things only to dismiss it as nonsense. "Altogether in the wrong are those who consider truth to be a property of being."[13] It appears that Spinoza was unfamiliar with

[9] "Quod autem a metaphysicis dici solet, ens unum et verum idem sunt, nugatorium et puerile est; quis enim nescit, hominem et unum hominem et vere hominem idem sonare." Hobbes, *Logica* 3, 7; *Opera philosophica* 1:32.

[10] Hobbes, *Logica* 3, 7; *Opera philosophica* 1:32.

[11] "He lacks all historical thinking, and has bequeathed to his followers the *mépris du passé*, causing much justified criticism." Willmann, *Idealismus* 3:251. "His letters consistently betray an arrogant contempt for Scholasticism. He had already thoroughly abandoned—unusual for his time—the manner of Scholastic reasoning and had followed his own trails. When the controversy with the Jesuits (1640) makes him realize the need to get better acquainted with Scholasticism, he confesses to Mersenne that he has not read any Scholastic writer in the last twenty years, and he only recalls the *Coimbricenses* as the authors of a Scholastic manual. He asks Mersenne's advice regarding any more recent pertinent work or brief compendium of Scholastic philosophy." Lasswitz, *Geschichte der Atomistik* 2:110.

[12] Willmann, *Idealismus* 3:241.

[13] "De Uno, Vero et Bono. Hi termini ab omnibus fere Metaphysicis pro generalissimis Entis affectionibus habentur; dicunt enim omne ens esse unum, verum et bonum, quamvis nemo de iis cogitet . . . apparebit ea [verum et fal-

the great thinkers of the Middle Ages;[14] not only that, he also may not have understood "the essential quest and ultimate concern" of an entire metaphysical tradition that enjoyed a revived interest in the Baroque era, Spinoza's own time.[15] Truth, he says, could only reside in a statement. Things, in contrast, he calls "mute"—a devastating notion that bespeaks abysmal consequences! The short chapter in the *Cogitata metaphysica* concludes thus: "Nothing more remains to be said. Even our preceding comments would not have been worthwhile except in view of those authors who at all cost had to search for the nodes on the rushes and wound up so entangled in such inanities that they could no longer find their way out."

---

sum] non nisi rerum denominationes extrinsecas esse neque rebus tribui, nisi rhetorice. . . . Prima igitur veri et falsi significatio ortum videtur duxisse a narrationibus: eaque narratio vera dicta fuisse, quae erat facti, quod revera contigerat: falsa vero, quae erat facti, quod nullibi contigerat. Atque hanc Philosophi postea usurparunt ad denotandum convenientiam idea cum suo ideato, et contra: quare idea vera dicitur illa, quae nobis ostendit rem, ut in se est: falsa vero, quae nobis ostendit rem aliter, quam revera est: Ideae enim nihil aliud sunt, quam narrationes sive historiae naturae mentales. Atque hinc postea metaphorice translata est ad res mutas, ut cum dicimus verum aut falsum aurum, quasi aurum nobis repraesentatum aliquid de seipso narret, quod in se est aut non est. Quocirca plane decepti sunt, qui verum terminum transcendentalem sive entis affectiones judicarunt. Nam de rebus ipsis non nisi improprie vel, si mavis, rhetorice dici potest . . . quare hic nihil restat notandum, nec etiam quae diximus operae pretium fuisset notare, si scriptores in similibus nugis non adeo se intricassent, ut postea se extricare nequiverint, nodum passim in scirpo quaerentes." Spinoza, *Cogitata* 1:6. Dunin-Borkowski, on the other hand, states: "Spinoza . . . worked under the assumption that the 'objective' essence of things, i.e., the objects in the act of their being known, coincides with the act of their being true and being real. This is the meaning of the statement, 'truth manifests itself'. . . . This 'objective' essence of things, however, is for Spinoza not a creation of the knowing subject. It is an essential property of the object known. As an aspect of reality, namely as knowability that by necessity becomes part of the act of knowing, it is of course inherent in the formal (physical) essence itself." Dunin-Borkowski, *Spinoza*, 65f. Cf. also Jansen, *Erkenntnislehre*, 115ff.

[14] This remains a strong probability, even though we cannot take as definite proof the fact alone that Spinoza's large library which he left behind "does not show any trace of the Christian Scholastics of the Middle Ages". Freudenthal, *Lebensgeschichte Spinozas*, 287.

[15] Dunin-Borkowski, *Spinoza*, 3:118.

We now look to *Leibniz* who, open-minded and knowledgeable, would not easily despise or dismiss traditional teachings. In his works we do find the general idea which is also expressed in the principle, "all that exists, is true". Yet here, elements of this idea are widely scattered, as it were, and hidden in various contexts. His doctrine of a primordial, predetermined universal harmony, the *consentement préétabli*, shows a certain affinity to the notion in question. Still, if we look for the formulation itself of the "truth of all things", which, of course, is no mere verbal construction but rather an expression whose very complexity of meaning indicates the universal reach of the cognitive connections involved, this formulation itself seems to be absent in Leibniz's vast and intricate opus.

We should not fail to mention here the opinion of some scholars who hold that Leibniz, contrary to his own words,[16] had "only superficial knowledge of thinkers like Albertus, Thomas, Bonaventure, or Scotus".[17] Noteworthy, too, is the way Leibniz's teacher, Jakob Thomasius, opens the chapter "on Truth" in his Latin catechism of "Metaphysical Questions": "Is truth, strictly speaking, a property of reality? No. Why not? Because truth does not reside in reality but in the mind that perceives reality. Can truth, therefore, in no wise be called a property of reality? Truth can be called an extrinsic, or an extrinsically defining, property of reality."[18]

---

[16] The *Discours de Métaphysique*, paragraph 11, mentions "my own research, which convinced me that we of this age are far from doing justice to Saint Thomas and the great masters of his time, and that the teachings of the Scholastic philosophers and theologians have much more substance than we commonly assume."

[17] Eschweiler, "Spanish Spätscholastic", 255: "It has been shown convincingly that this great poly-historian had only superficial knowledge of thinkers like Albertus, Thomas, Bonaventure, or Scotus. . . . In most instances it is evident that he used secondhand references to Thomas Aquinas' teachings, avoiding the time-consuming attempt to understand them within their proper context."

[18] Thomasius, *Erotemata*, chap. 5.

Kant, finally, long before the publication of the *Critique of Pure Reason*, labeled the principle of the truth of all things "sterile" and "tautological".[19] The 1781 first edition of the *Critique* is silent on this matter. The second edition, however, six years later, contains a newly inserted paragraph on the traditional doctrine of transcendentals, specifically on "what the Scholastics called the principle of the unity, truth, and goodness of all existing things".[20] There, we do indeed read:

> Now, although the application of this principle has proved very meager in consequences, and has indeed yielded only propositions that are tautological, and therefore in recent times has retained its place in metaphysics almost by courtesy only, yet, on the other hand, it represents a view which, however empty it may seem to be, has maintained itself over this very long period. It therefore deserves to be investigated in respect of its origin. . . .

Yet what results can we expect from such an investigation into the origins of a traditional ontological principle, after the entire thrust of philosophy had been reversed in Kant's "Copernican revolution"? He concludes that the principle of the truth (and unity and goodness) of all reality does definitely *not* indicate a "property of *things*"; its specific and valid meaning concerns, rather, "certain logical requirements and conditions inherent in any *perception* of things". The particular reasoning behind this interpretation is of no consequence for our topic here. For it becomes sufficiently clear already that Kant explicitly denies truth to be a property of reality as such. It is, therefore, entirely correct when certain approving commentators

[19] "Here we can consider three concepts together, the concepts of unity, truth, and perfection, because the respective propositions are, in themselves, empty. . . . It is the same regarding truth; for truth be in this: that every thing would be what it is—which is tautological as well." From one of Kant's manuscripts (ca. 1774), used for his lectures, quoted in Erdmann, "Mitteilungen", 81.

[20] Kant, *Kritik der reinen Vernunft*, paragraph 12 [quoted from Norman Kemp Smith's 1929 translation]. Regarding the history of this insertion, cf. Erdmann, "Mitteilungen", 8of.

see this paragraph of the *Critique* as intending to "discredit once and for all the basic concepts of traditional ontology".[21]

4

We should now try to find out in what form the basic concepts of traditional ontology had come to those philosophical innovators.

This much seems already certain: the above-mentioned philosophers of the seventeenth and eighteenth centuries, excepting Leibniz perhaps, did not know firsthand the great teachers of the High Middle Ages—Albertus Magnus, Thomas Aquinas, Duns Scotus—certainly not through those teachers' own texts and their own language. It is therefore quite possible that those latter-day philosophers took up arms against teachings that wrongly passed as "tradition" while not deserving that name. They might have fought a "tradition" whose ontological concepts, once keys to unlock reality, now had lost—if not their original meaning—at least their vigor, their freshness, their energy. We should not overlook the fact, however, that the authentic tradition flourished, undiminished and with renewed vitality, throughout the same time, the seventeenth century, and beyond. It flourished in the Scholasticism of the Baroque era, thanks in part to a small number of superior thinkers, but especially because of many outstanding and respected academic teachers, as Max Wundt has shown in an admirably precise and comprehensive study covering Protestant Germany.[22]

In which form, then, has someone like Immanuel Kant come to know the doctrine of the truth of all things? This question finds a rather precise answer. We know Kant's phi-

[21] "The entire transcendental analysis is directed against the teachings of traditional ontology. To discredit, once and for all, the basic concepts of traditional ontology is the purpose of this paragraph, and thus it rightly belongs in the *Critique of Pure Reason.*" Leisegang, *Behandlung,* 421.

[22] Wundt, *Schulmetaphysik.*

losophy teachers, Franz Albert Schulz and Martin Knutzen, who were disciples and followers of Christian Wolff, a philosopher of the German Enlightenment. Moreover, while teaching at the university, Kant selected as textbook for his obligatory lectures on metaphysics, even during the time the "Critiques" were published, the manual by Alexander Gottlieb Baumgarten, also a Wolff disciple. Wolff's *Philosophia prima sive Ontologia* and Baumgarten's *Metaphysica* (of exactly one thousand paragraphs) each contain a chapter dealing explicitly with the principle of the truth of all things.

We should mention right here that Wolff explains in a separate thesis his own notion of the universal truth of reality, as not standing against the teachings of the Scholastics, who, however, he says, had employed confusing terms, while his own formulations would define the concept with utmost precision. He evidently seeks legitimacy from the philosophical tradition, having asserted that he was more indebted to the works of Thomas Aquinas than to Leibniz's philosophy.[23] Strangely enough, people have believed him. The pertinent literature has consistently presented Wolff's philosophy as an authentic heir to the Scholasticism of the High Middle Ages.[24] The "concept of transcendentals" in particular, it is said, "had not changed at all".[25]

In truth, however, there exists hardly any affinity, much less a deeper agreement, between Wolff–Baumgarten and Albertus–Thomas–Scotus in their respective teachings on the truth of all things, despite terminological similarities. Actu-

[23] W. Schrader, in *Allgemeine deutsche Biographie* 44:14.
[24] Even the trusted custodians of the Scholastic tradition at times misunderstood him. Cf. Eschweiler, *Zwei Wege*, 81ff., 283, 296.
[25] Leisegang, *Behandlung*, 408. Schulemann, *Transzendentalien*, 71, writes: "The academic philosophy of the eighteenth century still follows [Suarez] often so closely that, e.g., Chr. Wolff's respective formulations, as we believe, can ultimately be traced back to him." Suarez should not simply and without qualification be considered equal to the great teachers of the High Middle Ages; yet even between him and Wolff there exist such basic differences, especially regarding the position on transcendentals (cf. chap. 4 notes), that here to speak of a "continuation of the tradition" is hardly justified.

ally, only someone lacking all sensitivity regarding levels of mental excellence can fail to recognize the abyss separating the intellectual giants of the High Middle Ages from the pedantic philosophical systematists of the Enlightenment.

5

First, then, we examine *Metaphysica* of *Baumgarten* for its stand on the doctrine of the truth of all things. The relevant statements are found in a chapter with five short Latin paragraphs[26] (the entire *Metaphysica* really is rather a "handy" handbook and not at all voluminous, despite its one thousand paragraphs).

The exposition begins by defining "transcendental truth"—an explanatory footnote in German calls this "the necessary metaphysical truth"—as the ordered structure governing the essential constituents and intrinsic attributes of all that exists, all being. The second paragraph states: "true" is a predicate of *all* that exists because the identifying dimensions of *every* being are, *in fact*, interconnected according to universal ordering principles. What could these ordering principles be? They are the following "universal principles" (*principia catholica*): the principle of contradiction (*principium contradictionis*): the principle of underlying reason (*principium rationis*);[27] distinct from the latter, the principle of sufficient reason (*principium rationis sufficientis*); finally, the *principium rationati*, difficult to translate, and meaning that no thing at all is ever totally superfluous and useless.[28] The third paragraph should be quoted verbatim: "*Confusio veritati transcendentali opposita esset somnium objective sumtum*" (with a footnote in German explaining, "ein Traum, das Geträumte"). "*Somnium aggregatum esset*

---

[26] Baumgarten, *Metaphysica*, sec. 6: "Verum"; paragraphs 89–93.

[27] Baumgarten elsewhere explains the *principium rationis* with these words: "Nihil est sine ratione, seu, posito aliquo, ponitur aliquid ejus ratio." *Metaphysica*, paragraph 20.

[28] Baumgarten, *Metaphysica*, paragraph 23.

mundus fabulosus" (footnote: "das Land der Wünsche"). Translated, it says: "The opposite of transcendental truth would be a dream mistaken for reality. A string of dreams would be a fairy tale world." The fourth paragraph contains a definition proper: "Metaphysical truth, therefore, is defined as the conformity of reality to the universal principles."[29] The last paragraph extends already beyond the subject matter of the chapter in question, as it deals with the concept of "certainty"; it thus lies outside our present interest.

What, then, is the core of this position? How is the principle of the truth of all things conceived here? That all that exists be real and not a dream! A dream, it says here, would differ from true reality in this: the latter conforms to the principles of contradiction and of sufficient reason and to the other "universal principles", while the shifting images of dreams escape the rules of logic and reality because they are not subject to the essential principles of knowledge and being.

It is hard to believe that such a meager result should constitute the sum total of those high-sounding paragraphs; hard to believe also that "Wolff's most important disciple"[30] should not in fact have intended to say something more profound. Yet, indeed, so it is.

After all, we should not expect even this disciple to be above his master. And his master's teachings, the statements of Christian *Wolff* himself, are certainly more original, as might be expected, but not at all more substantial. This can be shown with a few pertinent quotations:

---

[29] Baumgarten's disciple, Georg Friedrich Meier (1718–77), in his *Metaphysik* (4 vols., in German), also defines "metaphysical truth" as "conformity of reality to the universal principles of human cognition, i.e., to the principles of contradiction and of sufficient reason." Cf. Knittermeyer, *Terminus*, 197f. Meier's doctrine on reason provided a basis for Kant's lecture on logic. Cf. Überweg, *Geschichte* 3:459.

[30] Überweg, *Geschichte* 3:458. There, on p. 459, we also learn that Kant, "during his precritical period", considered Baumgarten "the most outstanding of contemporary metaphysicians."

The truth that is called "transcendental" and is conceived as inherent in reality as such . . . is the ordered structure governing
all existing things.[31] Truth is nothing else than the ordered
structure in the transformation of things; a dream, in contrast,
means inconsistency in the transformation of things.[32] The
truth implies order, the dream disorder.[33] The principle of
contradiction and the principle of sufficient reason are the well-
spring of the truth inherent in all things; which means: a thing
is true insofar as its essence is determined by those principles.
Consequently, should those principles, especially the latter,
ever disappear from the universe of all existing things, then the
real world would dissolve into a fairy tale (*mundus fabulosus*),
the equivalent of a dream.[34]

These statements are taken from Wolff's two main works,
*Vernünftige Gedanken von Gott, der Welt und der Seele des Men-
schen, auch allen Dingen überhaupt* [Reasonings on God, the
World and the Human Soul, also on All Things in General],
and *Philosophia prima sive Ontologia*. In these passages there
emerges a picture identical to the one in Baumgarten's *Metaphysica:* the truth of all things means simply that all existing
things are real, nothing more. The "reality" of a thing is defined as its conformity with "structured reason", which in
turn determines that "all instances of reality exist and occur
for a sufficient reason and do not leave room for inner
contradictions."[35]

This way of seeing all reality as "reasonable" is far removed
from Hegel's similar statement and even farther from the concept of "reason" as understood in the High Middle Ages
where its meaning was much broader than it is today.[36]
Christian Wolff, the "father of popular enlightenment in

---

[31] Wolff, *Philosophia prima*, paragraph 495.
[32] Wolff, *Vernünftige Gedanken*, pt. 1, paragraph 142.
[33] Wolff, *Philosophia prima*, paragraph 494.
[34] Wolff, *Philosophia prima*, paragraph 498.
[35] Wolff, *Philosophia prima*, paragraph 493.
[36] Cf. Pieper, *Zucht*, 26ff.

Germany",[37] quite clearly meant with "reality" and "being real" what the enlightened academic mentality of the time considered tangible, factual and objective. And "structured reason" here means no more than this: every thing has to make sense, all that exists and occurs has to have some rational explanation—otherwise it could not truly be real. We should also note in those texts the manifest contempt for dreams.

This is the same attitude that the young Goethe found prevalent in philosophical lectures of his time, an attitude he refused to accept. Stating later that "he had lacked any sense for philosophy proper, he only meant the bloodless school philosophy of the Wolffian kind."[38]

What, then, could be more justified than Kant's verdict on the doctrine of the truth of all things? In Wolff's and Baumgarten's interpretation it is indeed a sterile and empty tautology. Theirs is but a puny streamlet of a doctrine, studiously staked out, and deriving its undeniable clarity from nothing else than its lack of depth. There can be no comparison to the powerful original river of the old ontology, a river as limpid as it is profound, carrying in its swell even the sacred realities of mystery and dream!

6

His conception of the truth of all things, says Wolff, should be recognized as "distinct", in contrast to the Scholastics' conception, which he terms "confused".[39] This formulation is by no means insignificant or casual. The technical term "distinct" —meaning "sharply defined, precisely delineated"—has assumed a quite specific connotation since then, especially through Descartes. Wolff, without doubt, intended to convey fully this specific connotation in his remark. This matter deserves some closer investigation.

---

[37] Schöffler, *Deutscher Osten*, 199.
[38] Hildebrandt, *Goethe*, 28.
[39] Wolff, *Philosophia prima*, paragraph 502.

In the third of Descartes' *Meditations* we read: "I seem therefore justified in setting forth as a general principle that whatever I perceive 'clearly' and 'distinctly', is true."[40] With this
statement something unprecedented has occurred: the clarity
and precision of a concept has been made the criterion for its
factual truth. Still, what is a "distinct" concept? Descartes, in
his main work on the *Principles of Philosophy*, gives a meticulous description that has rightly been considered "of fundamental importance".[41] A "distinct" concept, according to
Descartes, is not only clear but, beyond that, is so different
and separated (*praecisa*) from any other concept that it contains
within itself nothing but what is clear.[42]

Wolff, therefore, labeling his own concept of truth "distinct" while denying this quality to the concept of the Scholastics, advances a quite ambitious claim. That the Scholastics
had only a confused notion of transcendental truth, Wolff
asserts, clearly emerges from "their inability to express this
notion in adequate terms".[43]

Certain proponents of Neoscholasticism, themselves
heavily influenced by Wolff's philosophy (as Eschweiler has
shown),[44] must have been quite perturbed when faced with
Wolff's assessment. Consequently, among the characteristics
of this brand of Neoscholasticism is the attempt to reinterpret
Thomas Aquinas in such a way as to attribute to this prophet
of the old ontology a position quite clearly stemming from the
rationalism of the Enlightenment: that it would be entirely
possible to grasp and explain the universe of all existing things
through textbook-style definitions, distinctions and demonstrations.

Yet Wolff, against Thomas, is right in this: the concept of
"truth" in classical Scholasticism is definitely not "distinct" in

[40] Descartes, *Meditationes*, pt. 3.
[41] Überweg, *Geschichte* 3:237.
[42] Descartes, *Principia* 1:45.
[43] Wolff, *Philosophia prima*, paragraph 502.
[44] Eschweiler, *Zwei Wege*, 81ff., 283, 296.

the Cartesian sense. More recent studies[45] have pointed to the obvious general unwillingness, also on the part of Thomas Aquinas, to advance a textbook definition of "truth" (and "knowledge" as well). For Thomas is well aware of the impossibility of capturing such primordial realities in this way. He therefore uses a different approach. In the opening *articulus* of the *Quaestiones disputatae de veritate*, entitled "What is Truth?", he first develops his own original conception, only to weave it then, with all modesty, into the strand of existing, traditional answers. He thus clarifies and explains his own and the traditional positions in mutual exchange. Not one answer is excluded, nor is any one answer accorded superiority. Although the quoted positions do not necessarily and easily harmonize with each other in all cases, he still upholds them all. Clearly, Thomas sees himself as a participant in a long and dynamic philosophical tradition. In the end, without claiming a final answer, he leaves the door wide open for further thought and exploration, not unlike Plato in his *Dialogues*.

We shall not dispute Wolff's assertion that he has the more "distinct" concept of truth. We feel entitled to doubt, however, that this more "distinct" concept would also be more adequate, more penetrating and more true.

7

In spite of the Scholastics' "confused" position, Wolff explains further, there could nevertheless be no mistake about their concept of truth being basically identical with his own,

---

[45] "Saint Thomas n'a pas accordé une importance extrême à la recherche d'une définition de la vérité; il est beaucoup plus préoccupé d'en dégager exactement la nature et les caractères que de l'enfermer dans une formule, quelque juste qu'elle soit." Kremer, "Synthèse", 319. "Thomas Aquinas does not attempt to come up with a textbook definition of the cognitive act itself; for he is keenly aware—correctly so, of course—that such a definition is not possible because it regards a primordial reality as, for example, the principle of contradiction, and such a reality can at best be described but not defined in any schoolmasterly manner." Hufnagel, *Studien*, 105. Cf. also Przywara, *Analogia*, 70ff, 124ff.

more "distinct" conception.[46] Wolff's concept may indeed be
more "distinct", but his claim of identity has to be rejected
emphatically—no matter whom he had in mind when referring to the "Scholastics": the German Protestant textbook
metaphysicians of the seventeenth century? or perhaps Suarez,
to whom he refers explicitly?[47] or the other Catholic Spaniards
of the Baroque era? or maybe even the great teachers of the
High Middle Ages,[48] whose rich substance provided suste-
nance for both groups mentioned, the Spanish and the German Protestant Scholastics? Since Wolff tries, with ample de-
scriptions, to identify his own position on "truth" specifically
with that of Suarez, we should point out that Suarez, as far as
our context here is concerned, stands solidly within the teachings of Thomas Aquinas.[49]

What, then, did Thomas Aquinas teach about the truth of
all things? To provide an answer to this question is the central
purpose of our study.

[46] "Etsi autem distinctam veritatis transcendentalis notionem tradere min-
ime potuerint, ea tamen tradidere, quae sufficiunt ad evincendam identitatem
notionis distinctae, quam nos dedimus, cum confusa, quae ipsis [= Scholas-
ticis] fuit." Wolff, *Philosophia prima*, paragraph 502.

[47] Wolff, *Philosophia prima*, paragraph 502.

[48] Wolff, in his autobiography (Wuttke, *Lebensbeschreibung*, 116), writes: "I
read Carboni's *Summa theologiae Thomae Aquinatis* so that I could thoroughly
get acquainted with catholic theology." It seems that Wolff was not familiar
firsthand with Thomas' writings. The book he mentions is probably an ep-
igone's compilation whose very title sounds presumptuous as it promises
what cannot be but facile and one-track answers, so alien to Thomas' mind.
In this, too, lies the difference between master and disciple. The full title
reads: "Compendium absolutissimum totius summae theologiae D. Thomae
Aquinatis, Doctoris Angelici. In quo universa ejus doctrina partim conclu-
sionibus quaestionum, partim vero argumentorum solutionibus, contenta
proponitur. Accuratissime omnia quae vel in sacris paginis obscura, vel in
gravissimis SS.PP. monumentis dubia, vel olim et hodie ab haereticis in con-
troversiam vocata, admirabili cum brevitate et claritate explicans. Auctore
R. D. Ludovico Carbone a Costaciario, SS. Theologiae in Gymnasio Pe-
rusino Professore", Köln, 1620. This book is not found in German libraries;
for the exact title I am indebted to Schöffler, *Deutscher Osten*, 185.

[49] Cf. the section on Suarez, in the notes for chap. 4, section 2.

Chapter Two

I

First and foremost, we quote Thomas Aquinas: "All existing things, namely, all real objects outside the soul, possess something intrinsic that allows us to call them true."[1] "In created things there is truth on two levels: in the things themselves, and in the perceiving mind."[2] Thomas, therefore, is not simply using "rhetoric", as Spinoza asserts,[3] when he calls the things themselves true. Quite on the contrary, he understands "the truth of all things" strictly literally.

Further: the things are true because of their essential reality of *being*. "Truth resides in the things and in the perceiving mind. The truth in the things, though, can also be called their being, according to the individual substance."[4] The truth of a thing is not some "property" that could equally be missing. Indeed, the reason for a thing's *being* is the same as for its *truth*. "We cannot perceive a thing to *be* without perceiving it to be *true*."[5] To what extent this thought is an integral part of the Western philosophical tradition may be seen in the fact that two diametrically opposed thinkers like Aristotle and Augustine (though they do not exclude each other) have formulated the same thought in almost identical expressions. The ancient Greek states: "As a thing relates to being, so also to truth",[6] while the Christian teacher at the end of antiquity writes: "Whatever is true has as much truth as it has being."[7] It seems

---

[1] "Res . . . quae est aliquid positivum extra animam, habet aliquid in se, unde vera dici possit." *Ver.* 1, 5 ad 2.

[2] "Veritas in creaturis invenitur in duobus, in rebus ipsis et in intellectu." *Ver.* 1, 6; cf. 1, 8.

[3] Spinoza, *Cogitata* 1:6. Cf. chap. 1, n. 13.

[4] "Verum est in rebus et in intellectu. Verum autem quod est in rebus, convertitur cum ente secundum substantiam." *ST* 1, 16, 3 ad 1.

[5] "Ens non potest intelligi sine vero." *Ver.* 1, 1 ad 3.

[6] Aristotle, *Metaphysics* 2, 1, 993b.

[7] Augustine, *De vera religione*, chap. 36.

noteworthy as well that the Indo-Germanic languages might originally have employed "true" [German: *wahr*] in the meaning of "to be".[8]

A thing cannot have *being* without equally having *truth*. *Est veritas in omnibus, quae sunt entia:* "Truth is found in all things inasmuch as they have being."[9] *Omnia res est vera et nulla res est falsa:* "All things are true and cannot be false."[10] Our perception can be true or false; the things themselves, however, are only and always true, never false. Truth is a *mode of being*, a mode that "pertains to every being as such"[11] and therefore embraces all categories and classes of being, "transcending" them. "Truth" is one of the universal "transcendental" terms applied to being as being.

In this respect, the term and concept of truth is coextensive with five further terms and concepts that Thomas Aquinas has set forth and explained in the first *articulus* of his *Quaestiones disputatae de veritate*. They are known as "transcendentals", a name given them later, and are listed as *ens, res, unum, aliquid, verum, bonum* [being, thing, oneness, identity, truth, goodness].

2

It is not too difficult to claim some initial and superficial understanding of these concepts. Their deeper meaning, though, the ultimate reality Thomas Aquinas intended to express, is not easily grasped by us moderns. Simply to analyze the paraphrase descriptive of these "transcendentals" in the hope of discovering their hidden meaning may not prove very helpful. It rather seems indispensable to enter first, deliberately and courageously, into the whole edifice of Thomas' world view.

---

[8] Friedrich Kluge, *Etymologisches Wörterbuch der deutschen Sprache*, 11th ed., Alfred Götze, ed. (Berlin, 1934).

[9] *Ver.* 1, 10.

[10] *Ver.* 1, 10.

[11] "Modus generaliter consequens omne ens." *Ver.* 1, 1.

From there, against the background of the whole, we may finally even more fully appreciate the extent of the initial question to which the "transcendentals" provide the answer.

Incidentally, those who have to rely on secondary sources face an additional difficulty here. The widely quoted "authority" and "standard source", C. Prantl's *Geschichte der Logik im Abendlande* [History of Logic in the West]—reprinted now again unaltered after one hundred years—treats our subject with almost grotesque inaccuracy. The common evaluation of this study as "admirably informed" and "meticulously presenting its sources"[12] must be rejected emphatically. One is led to assume that Prantl, on the contrary, was not even superficially familiar with the works of someone like Thomas Aquinas.[13] What he presents as quotations from Thomas ex-

[12] Heinrich Scholz, *Logik*, p. v. The most recent comprehensive history of logic, however, speaks of Prantl thus: "It would be better to disregard him entirely. A modern historian of logic is led, unfortunately, to consider him altogether irrelevant. He is disproved, incidentally, by the unanimous results of recent research." Bochenski, *Formale Logik*, 10.

[13] One example here should suffice: Even beginners know that the Scholastic *articulus* consists of three parts. The main part is the one in the middle, the *corpus articuli*, in which the matter in question is discussed systematically. The preceding first part always lists a number of "objections", i.e., arguments (sometimes, especially in more extensive *Quaestiones disputatae*, even counterarguments) taken from literary sources, supporting or denying the thesis treated in the *corpus*. These objections, one by one, are then dealt with in the third part, following the *corpus* of the *articulus*. Thus, the respective author himself speaks only in parts two and three of the *articulus*; only the *corpus* and the answers to the objections reflect his own position. The first part, the objections, are but citations that as a rule present opinions explicitly rejected by the author himself. Prantl now, in his discussion of Thomas Aquinas (vol. 3, p. 114), quotes several passages taken from these objections, yet assuming to present Thomas' own opinion. Prantl thus attributes to Thomas positions explicitly rejected by Thomas.

One of the objections quoted by Prantl (*Ver.* 1, 1, contr. 4) refers to the Neoplatonic *Liber de causis*, whose origins incidentally, unknown for a long time, had been "discussed in the Middle Ages by none more clearly than by Thomas" (Baeumker, *Witelo*, 189). The other objection quoted by Prantl (*Ver.* 1, 1 contr. 5) relates the concepts of *ens, unum, verum, bonum* in a certain way to the Trinity.

Prantl explains first that Thomas "knew only those four concepts", while the full number of six transcendentals would appear "for the first time" in *De*

presses Thomas' true position no better, in fact much less, than the obtuse remarks of the servant Wagner in *Faust* express the wisdom of Goethe. And yet, those quotations, together with Prantl's disparaging appraisals, have now for several generations been repeated over and over in countless treatises, causing widespread and almost incurable errors. [14]

It is impossible for our present study on transcendental truth to deal in any depth with the other transcendentals as well and to show their more profound significance. A brief sketch of their general meaning will have to suffice here. The term *ens*, being, shall not receive at this time any further explanation.

Res: there is no adequate translation for this term. It has been called a Latin "core term", a gift from the Romans to the entire world. [15] The meaning of *res* covers an extensive realm of "things", including material possessions, juridical claims, historical events, public order, the commonwealth—and, of course, things, objects, reality. From *res* comes our "real" and the German *reell* [true, honest]. There is, indeed, nothing that could not be labeled *res*. The term "thing", in contrast, cannot

---

natura generis, a treatise judged by Prantl to be post-thomistic, even post scotistic (vol. 3, p. 245). Yet Thomas, in fact, explicitly and extensively treats precisely all those six transcendentals in the *corpus* of the same *articulus* from which Prantl had taken the objections. Those six concepts, moreover, constitute the formal and exclusive subject of this *articulus*. It should be noted here, in passing, that recent research (e.g., Grabmann, *Werke*, 354ff.) attributes the treatise *De natura generis* also to Thomas himself.

Prantl, then, based on his entirely inaccurate premise, concludes that Thomas, "led astray by the mysticism of the *Liber de causis*, used its four concepts of *ens, unum, verum* and *bonum* for a theological purpose and thus corrupted genuine Aristotelianism and Platonism" (vol. 3, p. 114). The truth is that Thomas in his answer to the respective objection (*Ver.* 1, 1 ad 5, contr.), specifically rejects any attempt to relate the transcendentals to the Trinity and never mentions the *Liber de causis* at all.

[14] Prantl's false quotations from Thomas reappear, e.g., in Knittermeyer, *Terminus*, an otherwise quite excellent and independent study (independent even from Prantl). Schulemann, *Transzendentalien*, also lacks a sufficiently critical approach to Prantl's book.

[15] Theodor Haecker, *Vergtil, Vater des Abendlandes* (Leipzig, 1931), 117ff.

be applied with such ease to just anything there is. More comprehensive and more general, more in line with the latitude of
res, may be "whatsoever" [German: *was*], but it lacks the linguistic position and power of *res*. Thomas uses *res* to indicate
the root of an entity's being. The term *ens*, being, is a parti-
ciple pointing to the *act* of being, whereas *res* specifically
means the *subject* sustaining this act.[16]

Unum: each existing thing is "one" or intrinsically "unified". For Thomas, transcendental unity means that a thing in
its being is not divided into parts. "The being of any existing
thing is sustained inasmuch as it is not divided into parts. Each
thing, therefore, as it guards its being, so also guards its intrinsic oneness."[17] We moderns find it particularly difficult to
grasp the basic thrust and specific significance of this thought.
Suffice it to point out that Thomas uses an entity's greater or
lesser oneness, the degree of its intrinsic unity, as criterion to
establish the hierarchy of beings. A plant enjoys greater oneness than a rock; an animal is more "intrinsically one" than a
plant; a spirit-endowed person represents the highest level of
"intrinsic oneness"; and God is the ultimate perfection of
"Oneness": *Deus est maxime unus.*[18]

Aliquid: every existing being is *aliquid*. This statement is not
as plain and definitely not as tautological as it may at first appear. The common translation of *aliquid* with "something"
would be quite misleading here. For the meaning of *aliquid*,
explained already in medieval etymology (we may add, correctly, for once),[19] is the same as *aliud quid*, "something other,
something apart". Every existing thing is "something apart",
which means: something distinguished and separated from all

[16] "Ens sumitur ab actu essendi, sed nomen rei exprimit quidditatem sive
essentiam entis." *Ver.* 1, 1.

[17] "Unde manifestum est quod esse cujuslibet rei consistit in indivisione.
Et inde est quod unumquodque sicut custodit suum esse, ita custodit suam
unitatem." *ST* I, 11, 1.

[18] *ST* I, 11, 4. Regarding the problem of ontological "unity", cf. Oeing-
Hanhoff, *Ens et unum.*

[19] "Dicitur enim aliquid quasi aliud quid." *Ver.* 1,1.

other things, something with its own identity.[20] This transcendental concept of *aliquid*, just about forgotten in later
Scholastic tradition, thus opens an illuminating approach to
reality, illuminating as much in breadth as in depth: all that exists, exists as form; all form in turn is defined by its delimitation. This concept of "delimitation" of one thing against the
other is intimately connected, on a linguistic level, with primordial existential terms, as German linguistics, surprisingly
and convincingly, has shown some time ago.[21]

The transcendentals *ens, res* and *unum* regard the intrinsic reality of all that is, as distinct froin *aliquid*, which implies an essential relatedness of every being to another being.[22] In this,
the concept of *aliquid* resembles the concepts of "truth" and
"goodness". A specific kind of relatedness, in fact, is stated by
the two principles of the truth and the goodness[23] of all existing things, namely, that every being is oriented toward a
knowing and loving (that is, willing) mind.

3

We now return to the more limited field of our specific topic,
after having received a preliminary answer to our question regarding the actual disposition of what is called the truth of all
things. *Verum importat ordinem quemdam entis ad intellectum;*[24]
verum habet ordinem ad cognitionem:[25] "all things are true"
means they are oriented toward a knowing self.

---

[20] "Sicut ens dicitur unum, inquantum est indivisum in se, ita dicitur aliquid, inquantum est ab aliis divisum." *Ver.* 1, 1.

[21] We wish to refer to the publications by Jost Trier, especially the study,
First. Über die Stellung des Zauns, and the article, "Zaun und Mannring".

[22] "Modus generaliter consequens omne ens . . . dupliciter accipi potest:
uno modo secundum quod consequitur omne ens in se, alio modo secundum
quod consequitur unumquodque ens in ordine ad aliud." *Ver.* 1, 1.

[23] The significance of the principle *ens et bonum convertuntur* is thoroughly
explained in Lotz, *Sein und Wert*.

[24] *De natura generis*, chap. 2.

[25] *ST* I, 16, 3.

To sum up what was stated so far: truth is predicated of every being inasmuch as it has being. And this truth is seen as actually residing *in* all things, so much so that "truth" may interchangeably stand for "being". And further, the truth of all things is coextensive with the very being of all things; for there is no being at all that would not, by necessity, also be true. All this, then, has some immediate implications: every being, as being, stands in relation to a knowing mind. This relational orientation toward a knowing mind represents the same ontological reality as the very being of a thing. "To be", therefore, means the same as "to be oriented toward a knowing mind". The realm of "being as such", finally, does not extend beyond the realm of all that is oriented toward a knowing mind, so that no existing being is without such relational orientation. "Nothing can be perceived as 'being' and not at the same time as 'true'. For no real 'being' can be perceived without implying that it relates or 'conforms' to the knowing mind."[26]

With all "being" thus related to a knowing mind, we further state that this relationship is actualized in the process of mental perception or intellection. "The mind's act of intellection itself constitutes and completes that relation of 'conformity' which is the nature of all truth."[27]

4

It would be improper, however, and indeed at this point of our study not only misleading or, as it were, tactically unwise but outright mistaken, to declare that the truth of all things would be nothing else than their being known. Instead, and first of all, we have to show decisively that the concepts of "intellection" and "knowledge" are employed by classical

---

[26] "Ens non potest intelligi sine vero, quia ens non potest intelligi sine hoc, quod correspondeat vel adaequetur intellectui." *Ver.* 1, 1 ad 3.

[27] "In ipsa operatione intellectus . . . completur relatio adaequationis, in qua consistit ratio veritatis." *Sent.* 1, 19, 5, 1.

Scholasticism in a much broader sense compared to their customary usage. We may generally understand mental perception and knowledge as a process whereby the mind reproduces within itself the external world. The Middle Ages, however, added to this conception a whole further dimension, including in it, for example, the notion of "creative knowledge". (This notion of "creative knowledge" has by now been quite distorted through extensive misapplication. It ought to be stated right here that it must not be interpreted as declaring the very act of intellection, and therefore all knowledge as such, to be "creative". On the contrary, it simply says that there exists, beside and beyond noncreative knowing, a specific kind of knowing that bestows on the objects thus "known" their respective being.)

We have to return to the roots in order to find out how the Middle Ages, how great teachers like Thomas Aquinas, addressing an as yet unfragmented Western Christendom, have determined the nature of knowledge.

To begin with, we have to point out that Thomas Aquinas, once again and deliberately, has not provided a definition proper of his conception regarding the mind's ability to know. Through various approaches, employing at least ten different terms, he has tried to stake out and delineate the essential nature of knowledge, all the while "fully convinced that none of these concepts could ever adequately define the nature of intellection".[28] We may quote here the strikingly appropriate remark by a Thomist philosopher who comments on the critical approach of modern epistemology: to have discovered the dimension of mystery in all our knowing, he says, "is about the only genuine finding of all modern theory of knowledge".[29]

---

[28] Hufnagel, *Studien*, 105. Hufnagel, in his impressive study, identifies and discusses the following terms, all used by Thomas to describe the act of knowing: *operatio, actio, motus, generatio, formatio, assimilatio, unio, perfectio, vita.*

[29] Przywara, *Ringen* 1:263.

"Beings endowed with the ability to know are distinct from
those not so endowed inasmuch as the latter do not have any
other form but their own, while the former are capable of having also the form of the other being"—so we read in the
Summa theologica of Thomas Aquinas.[30]

We can give only a brief comment on this. "Form" stands
for that which gives a thing its identity, which makes it what
it is. The "form" of a thing is its intrinsic identifying imprint,
so that every thing is what it is through the "form" it "has".

For a thing to have knowledge, then, means to carry in itself
the identity (*quidditas*) of some other being or thing, and not
only its "image" but indeed its "form". A being's ability to
know, therefore, is its ability to transcend its own delimita-
tions, the ability to step out of its own identity and to have
"also the form of the other being", which means: to *be* the
other being.[31] "Knowing" constitutes and establishes the
most intimate relationship conceivable between two beings (a
fact that is expressed and confirmed through the age-old usage
of "knowing" to indicate sexual intercourse).

To sum it up: all that has being also has truth. The truth of
a being consists in its orientation toward a knowing mind.
And this cognitive relationship between mind and reality is actualized by the mind's "having" the essential form of an existing thing. Therefore, the principle of the truth of all existing
things means specifically this: it belongs to the inherent nature
of any existing thing that its essential form (by which a thing
is what it is) is actually or potentially "received" by a knowing
self; and further, that any thing's essence, thus "received", is
actually or potentially owned, even absorbed, by the knowing
mind. All reality is actually or potentially mind-related, inasmuch as its intrinsic essence is actually or potentially incorporated into the knowing mind.

[30] "Cognoscentia a non cognoscentibus in hoc distinguuntur, quia non
cognoscentia nihil habent nisi formam suam tantum; sed cognoscens natum est
habere formam etiam rei alterius." *ST* I, 14, 1. Cf. *ST* I, 80, 1 and *Ver.* 2, 2.
[31] Cf. Pieper, *Reality and the Good*, chap. 1, below.

5

The mind perceives a thing by way of participation in its intrinsic nature, and this participation is conceived by Thomas
Aquinas as a relationship of actual identity between mind and
objective being.[32] The order of priority in this relationship,
then, can flow either from the object or from the knowing
mind, as the identity of form can be constituted and determined either beginning with the object or with the mind.

To bring this into focus, however, a distinction has to be
made. If the relationship of participation and identity between
mind and object is considered under the aspect of its existence
as such, its general reality, its actual presence, then this relationship arises always and exclusively from the mind, not
from the object. For it is the mind that initiates this relationship; the objects on their own do not establish a relationship
to the perceiving mind. As Thomas puts it: it is always the
mind's act of intellection that "constitutes and completes" the
correlation between mind and reality.[33]

The situation is different, though, if in this relationship of
identity between material object and knowing mind we do
not consider its existence as such but its essence, not "that" it
is but "what" it is, not its being-there but its being-such, not
its fact but its content. For within this correlation of identity
thus considered, either the mind or the object can each impose
the "measure" as well as receive the "measure".[34] Within this
correlation of formal identity, either the object provides the

---

[32] Pieper, *Reality and the Good*, 115.

[33] Cf. the statement quoted in n. 27.

[34] "The concept of 'measure' has to be approached from the concept of 'essential form'. The 'measure' of an existing thing is its 'extrinsic' form; it is—as
in Meister Eckhart—the 'preceding type', and thus, in a very direct sense, the
'archetype' of reality. The essential form inherent in a thing is, for Scholasticism, its 'intrinsic formal cause'; the 'measure' of a thing is its 'extrinsic formal cause', which—together with the intrinsic formal cause, yet preceding it-
—causes the thing to be what it is." Pieper, *Reality and the Good*, see below
109f.; further details can be found there as well.

original form with the mind being in-formed, or, conversely, the mind provides the original form with the object being in-formed.

Here, then, we have the foundation on which rests the distinction between *intellectus speculativus* and *intellectus practicus*, between the mind's two modes of knowing: contemplative and receptive, or causative and formative.

> Reality compares differently to either the active way of knowing or the receptive way of knowing. The mind in its active intellection is the cause of things, and therefore is the "measure" of those things it produces. The mind in its receptive intellection, on the other hand, is the receiver of things, and is in some sense activated by them; those things, therefore, are then the "measure" of the mind. [35]

Be it emphasized concerning this distinction that the *intellectus practicus* is equally seen as true *intellectus*, as genuine power of cognition. *Intellectus practicus veritatem cognoscit sicut speculativus:* active intellection perceives truth as well as receptive intellection. [36] The *intellectus practicus*, too, stands in a true relation of knowing to those realities that receive from it their "measure", meaning: their specific nature. Thomas Aquinas speaks of certain things that are "essentially designed to spring from the knowledge of a mind". [37]

The power of the mind's active intellection to create and cause reality, however, covers only the specific nature and not the very being of things thus "known". It is from the creative *will* "that" a thing is; it is the creative *intellection* that deter-

---

[35] *Ver.* 1, 2. *Ver.* 3, 3, ad 5 is only an apparent contradiction.

[36] *ST* I, 79, 11 ad 2.

[37] *Ver.* 3, 3. This passage directly discusses the distinction between *cognitio speculativa* and *cognitio practica*. The first exists "quando nullo modo est ad actum ordinabilis cognitio". Yet this can happen in two ways: "uno modo, quando cognitio est de rebus illis, quae non sunt natae produci per scientiam cognoscentis, sicut nos cognoscimus naturalia. . . ."

mines "what" a thing is.[38] The mind, by its creative knowledge, produces in itself the essential form of certain things.
This prescriptive, creative knowledge makes the knowing
mind — or rather the paradigmatic form produced in the
mind — the "measure" of reality.[39] In and through creative
knowledge is the intrinsic form of an artistic or technical work
"thought out" and, as concept, given existence.[40] This form,
in turn, this *forma praeconcepta*,[41] in order to be transformed
into factual reality, needs the determination of the will and the
skill of the hands.

6

The correlation between reality and the creative intellection of
the mind, a correlation in which all the specifics of an object
depend in their existence on the mind, constitutes indeed the
fullest and most genuine of all relationships between mind and
reality. No other thing do we know as thoroughly as the creation of our own mind and our own hands — provided it is
truly our own creation. "An object that is known can be oriented toward the knowing mind either in an intrinsic or in an
accidental relationship. An intrinsic relationship exists when
the object, in its being, depends on the knowing mind; an accidental relationship, in contrast, exists when the object is

---

[38] "Artifex per ordinem suae sapientiae et intellectus artificiata in esse pro-
ducit. Ergo et Deus omnes creaturas per ordinem sui intellectus facit." *CG* 2,
24. "Deus facit creaturam ut agens per intellectum." *CG* 2, 25. "Unius et
ejusdem effectus, etiam in nobis, est causa scientia ut dirigens, qua concipitur
forma operis; et voluntas ut imperans: quia forma, ut est in intellectu tantum,
non determinatur ad hoc quod sit vel non sit in effectu, nisi per voluntatem."
ST I, 19, 4 ad 4.

[39] Pieper, *Reality and the Good*, 109.

[40] Active intellection is accomplished through two different *habitus:* that of
artistry or that of prudence. The first is for Thomas *recta ratio factibilium*, the
latter *recta ratio agibilium*. Cf. *ST* II, 1, 57, 4. Also Pieper, *Klugheit*, 58. On the
"truth" in morality, cf. Ermecke, *Seinsgrundlagen*, 59ff.

[41] "Sicut artifex praeconcepta forma proponit illam in materiam in-
ducere . . . ." *Ver.* 3, 3.

merely perceived by the mind."[42] The essential form of a statue, for example, lives most vividly and lucidly in the artist's mind (again, *inasmuch* as the sculpture is the creation of the artist; the marble is someone else's work). And in the conception of an inventor and builder — *as far as* being an original idea — a machine exists as much as in the eye of its operator, even more so. The creatively knowing mind of the artist (or technician) is present in the objective, material work as intimately as conversely the work is present in the mind of its creator.

A relation of mental perception in the more literal, limited sense is, of course, also contained in such mutual cognitive indwelling; yet at the same time it is extended by a further dimension. The knowing perception that is directed "toward things not designed to be brought into existence by the knowledge of a mind, the way we perceive the objects of nature"[43] — this perception in the more restricted sense is indeed equally actualized in the relationship between the artist and his work. The objectively and materially existing work of art is "known" by the artist also in the way he knows "the objects of nature". Yet he knows it more intensely than he could ever know and understand, say, a tree or any other reality not created by him. (On the other hand, a finite mind will never achieve "understanding", in the full and precise meaning of the term,[44] not even understanding of its own creation. For this would require the impossible precondition that such a mind have perfect understanding of itself.)

---

[42] "Res intellecta ad intellectum aliquem potest habere ordinem vel per se vel accidens. Per se quidem habet ordinem ad intellectum, a quo dependet secundum suum esse. Per accidens autem ad intellectum, a quo cognoscibilis est." *ST* I, 16, 1.

[43] *Ver.* 3, 3.

[44] "Someone would 'understand' a thing in the full meaning of the word if he could understand it as perfectly as it is understandable in itself." *Joh.* I, 11.

"The forms conceived by the receptive mind are the foundation of knowing only, while the forms conceived by the active mind are the foundations of both knowing and being."[45]

7

Only apparently have we strayed from the direct path of our inquiry. We need make but one step in order to regain our trail.

If the truth of an existing thing consists in its orientation toward the knowing mind, and if the relationship between material object and knowing mind finds its fullest and most genuine actualization in the correlation between the creative mind and its creation, then this conclusion follows: "True in an absolute sense are all things insofar as they are ordered toward the knowing mind on which their being depends."[46] Truth in its most authentic meaning, therefore, is predicated of an objective reality insofar as this reality's intrinsic form is patterned after some preceding original form residing in a creatively knowing mind.

> And so do we call all manufactured things "true" because of their orientation toward our knowing mind. We can call a house "true" inasmuch as it conforms to the original idea in the mind of the architect. And a speech can be called "true" insofar as it reveals a true thought. And similarly are the things of nature called "true" as they mirror their primordial forms, which dwell in the mind of God.[47]

[45] "Unde nihil prohibet formas intellectus speculativi esse tantum principia cognoscendi; formas autem intellectus practici esse principia essendi et cognoscendi simul." *Ver.* 3, 3 ad 7.

[46] *ST* I, 16, 1.

[47] "Et inde est, quod res artificiales dicuntur verae per ordinem ad intellectum nostrum. Dicitur enim domus vera, quae assequitur similitudinem formae quae est in mente artificis; et dicitur oratio vera, inquantum est signum intellectus veri. Et similiter res naturales dicuntur esse verae, secundum quod assequuntur similitudinem specierum, quae sunt in mente divina." *ST* I, 16, 1.

8

What, then does the principle of the truth of all things specifically affirm? The orientation toward the creative knowledge of a *finite* mind (though such a mind may well be capable of creative knowledge) does not apply universally to the *totality* of all existing things. Consequently, we have to state: the principle of transcendental truth means primarily that all existing beings are ordered toward the creative knowledge of *God's* mind. This is indeed an important first conclusion regarding the meaning of the principle in question, although this conclusion does not yet satisfy our anthropological interest. "And thus are 'being' and 'truth' interchangeable, *because* every thing in the world, by its intrinsic form, conforms to God's artistry",[48] as Thomas Aquinas formulates this teaching in his late, unfinished commentary on Aristotle's treatise *Peri hermeneias*.

The truth of all things, understood as their foundation in the "artistry" of God, implies a twofold affirmation. First, all things are known by God.[49] This statement, to be accessible and comprehensible in its full depth, has to be stripped of its common, already quite tiresome moralizing overtones. It says that no existing being is intrinsically "irrational", unknowable (indeed: unknown) or obscure. And this teaching that all things are "known" by God is by no means simply an inconsequential notion within the confines of theology. Indeed, reality itself takes on a different character depending on whether a person accepts this teaching.

---

[48] "Ens et verum convertuntur, quia quaelibet res naturalis per suam formam arti divinae comparatur." *Periherm.* 1, 5. The Middle Ages employed the term *ars* [art: "Kunst"] not so much for the entire area of artistic production and objective works of art, as we do today, but primarily and more specifically for the inner disposition of the artist himself, his artistry, which prompts him to be creative.

[49] "Nulla res est quam intellectus divinus actu non cognoscat." *Ver.* 1, 2 ad 4.

God's knowledge, however, is creative—the second affirmation. Augustine, in the last chapter of his *Confessions*,[50] states that we see things because they exist, but they exist only because God sees them. A great literary work of our own time expresses the same thought:

> For all things exist only as seen by Thee,
> Only as known by Thee, all things exist
> Only in Thy light . . . .
>   T. S. Eliot, *Murder in the Cathedral*, closing chorus

We are not simply declaring here, strictly speaking, that God has created everything out of nothing. Rather, we intend to say, using an image from ancient Egyptian ontology,[51] that everything has sprung from God's *eye*. And this means that the primordial forms of all things reside in the creative mind of God, that the intrinsic forms of all things are "nothing else but God's knowledge somehow imprinted (*sigillatio*) in those things'.[52] This, too, determines a very specific *world view*, because something about reality as such is being affirmed. "Truth, as predicated of all things in their relation to God's knowing mind, is an inherent and inseparable quality."[53] Does it not entail a decisive difference in a person's philosophy of life whether this statement of Thomas Aquinas is accepted or not: "The things are more in God than God is in the things"?[54] Some further passages from Thomas shall be quoted here, similarly expressing the doctrine that all things are rooted in the knowing mind of God. "Since all things, created by God, dwell in God inasmuch as they are known by him, it follows that all things in him are part of his divine

---

[50] Augustine, *Confessions* 12, 38; cf. also *De Trinitate* 6, 10.

[51] Willmann, *Idealismus* 1:51.

[52] "Sicut scientia in nobis est sigillatio rerum in animabus nostris, ita e converso formae non sunt nisi quaedam sigillatio divinae scientiae in rebus." *Ver.* 2, 1 ad 6.

[53] "Veritas quae dicitur de eis (= rebus) in comparatione ad intellectum divinum, eis inseparabiliter communicatur." *Ver.* 1, 4.

[54] "Magis res sunt in Deo quam Deus in rebus." *ST* I, 8, 3 ad 1.

life."⁵⁵ "The essence even of a lifeless thing has life in God's mind."⁵⁶ And in the commentary on John, regarding the passage in the Prologue, "All that was made was life in him", we read:

All existing things can be considered in two ways, either as they are in themselves or as they are in the Word. Considered in themselves, not all things constitute life nor are they alive; for some things are inanimate, others are living beings. The earth, for instance, was made, as also were the metals, and neither is life nor has life. The animals were made, human beings were made, and it is not that in themselves they are life, they simply have life. Yet if things are considered as they are in the Word, then they not only have life, they are life. For the original essence of every existing thing dwells as idea in God's wisdom; this essence constituted the pattern by which the Word created a particular thing; and this essence is life. Thus a precious vessel, created by an artist, in itself neither is life nor has life. The original idea of the vessel, however, previously conceived in the artist's mind, in a certain sense has life insofar as it lives as ideal knowledge in the artist's mind. Not that it *is* life; for even though it is known by the artist, it is not intrinsically part of his nature nor of his being. With God this is different: God's knowing *is* his life and his nature; and so, whatever is in God, not only *has* life but really *is* life, because whatever is in God belongs to his nature. Consequently, any created thing dwells in God as creative essence. If, then, all existing things are considered as they are in the Word, they indeed *are* life.⁵⁷

⁵⁵ "Cum omnia, quae facta sunt a Deo, sint in ipso ut intellecta, sequitur quod omnia in ipso sunt ipsa vita divina." *ST* I, 18, 4.

⁵⁶ "Et rationes rerum, quae in seipsis non vivunt, in mente divina sunt vita." *ST* I, 18, 4 ad 2.

⁵⁷ "Res enim dupliciter considerari possunt, secundum scilicet quod sunt in seipsis, et secundum quod sunt in Verbo. Si considerentur secundum quod sunt in seipsis, sic non omnes res sunt vita nec etiam viventes. Sed aliquae carent vita, aliquae vivunt. Sicut facta est terra, facta sunt etiam metalla, quae nec vita sunt nec vivunt. Facta sunt animalia, facti sunt homines, quae secundum quod sunt in seipsis, non sunt vita, sed vivunt solum. Si vero considerentur secundum quod sunt in Verbo, non solum sunt viventes, sed etiam vita. Nam rationes Dei spiritualiter existentes, quibus res factae sunt ab ipso Verbo, sunt vita. Sicut arca facta per artificem se quidem nec vivit nec vita est; ratio vero

All this, of course, is nothing else but the repetition of the classical Western doctrine of the *Ideas*, which in fact states that the archetypes, the ideas, of all existing things subsist in God; and that all created things "mirror the essence of God . . . in different ways and degrees";[58] and that, further, "the divine essence, insofar as it can be mirrored by a specific reality in a specific manner, constitutes the very nature and idea of this reality."[59] It should also have become apparent to the extent this doctrine of *Ideas* is connected with the doctrine of the *Logos*, a core subject of Christian speculation in the West. It is interesting to note that Augustine even calls the *Logos* the "artistry" of God,[60] an expression taken up, in the Middle Ages, especially by Bonaventure whose reflections undergirded and developed it further.[61]

9

Admittedly, as already mentioned, this preliminary description of the concept of transcendental truth does not specifically satisfy our anthropological inquiry. Still, there should not be the slightest doubt that the rather theological aspect of the doctrine about the truth of all things is intimately tied to its

---

arcae, quae praecessit in mente artificis, vivit quodammodo, inquantum habet esse intelligibile in mente artificis; non tamen est vita, quia per ipsum intelligere artificis non est in sua essentia neque suum esse. In Deo autem suum intelligere est sua vita et sua essentia: et ideo quidquid est in Deo, non solum vivit, sed est ipsa vita, quia quidquid est in Deo, est sua essentia. Unde creatura in Deo est creatrix essentia. Si ergo considerentur res secundum quod in Verbo sunt, vita sunt." *Joh.* 1, 2.

[58] "Licet omnes res, inquantum sunt, divinam essentiam imitentur, non tamen uno et eodem modo omnia imitantur ipsam, sed diversimode et secundum diversos gradus." *Quol.* 4, 1.

[59] "Sic ergo divina essentia, secundum quod est imitabilis hoc modo ab hac creatura, est propria ratio et idea hujusmodi creaturae." *Quol.* 4, 1.

[60] "Verbum perfectum . . . et ars quaedam omnipotentis atque sapientis Dei, plena omnium rationum viventium incommutabilium." Augustine, *De Trinitate* 6, 10.

[61] Primarily in his Commentary on the Sentences of Peter Lombard (I, 31, 2, 2) and in the treatise on the Six Days of Creation (I, 13).

anthropological aspect. It may also be pointed out that the anthropological aspect of this doctrine could not have been con-
structed except on the very same theological foundation. And
if in the philosophy of the Enlightenment the doctrine of the
truth of all things has indeed degenerated into a stale and sterile tautology, devoid of any real message, then the main reason may well be that the original, first and foremost theological meaning of that traditional ontological principle had been
ignored or forgotten. The leading historian of philosophical
Idealism, Otto Willmann, identifies the situation accurately
when he says that "as the Ideas are thrown out, there also go
the transcendentals".[62]

10

We shall stay just a bit longer with the more theological aspect
of our subject; for we wish to point briefly—almost as an in-
terlude—to a characteristic trait contained in the concept of
God as this concept emerges from what we have said so far
about the doctrine of the *Ideas* and of the truth of all things.

   Toward the end of the eighteenth century there occurred in
Germany a controversy, sometimes called "the German pan-
theism dispute",[63] which was to have important consequences
for German philosophy. Participants in this controversy, including Lessing, Herder, Kant, Goethe, and Jacobi, tried to
formulate their position with regard to what was then called
Spinozism. Within this dispute, the concept of a God "outside
this world", considered orthodox Christian teaching by proponents and opponents alike, played a significant and even
fateful role (fateful, because in this way the *genuine* tradition of
Western Christianity was not represented). "You are . . . a
true orthodox Christian; for you profess a God who is outside
this world, as is right and proper"—so, for example, writes

---

[62] Willmann, *Idealismus* 3:583.
[63] Hildebrandt, *Goethe*, 200ff.; Hettner, *Literatur* 3:44ff.

Herder[64] to Jacobi, who in this dispute thinks to defend the teachings of Christianity. Here also do we find the context for Goethe's later poem:

> What god at work in outer space would linger
> And let the universe spin round his finger!
> Fitter it is, He'd give things inward motion
> Fill Self and World with mutual devotion,
> That all which in Him lives and weaves and grows
> His power and His spirit shares and knows.[65]

Our own time seems willing enough, without much reflection, to take the concept of an "outside" God for orthodox Christian teaching—again, as do opponents and proponents of this concept alike. But how could this allegedly Christian concept of God be reconciled with the conception held by the great Christian thinkers of the High Middle Ages—Thomas Aquinas, for instance? He maintained, as we have seen in his doctrine on the truth of all things, that the archetypes of all things, and the things themselves, are in God,[66] while God "is necessarily in all things, in the most intrinsic manner".[67] Thomas Aquinas would never speak of an "outside" God. It is one thing to affirm that Creator and creation are not identical, or to hold that God transcends the knowing power of any finite mind. But to speak of a *Deus extramundanus* [a God outside the world] is not the Christian language; it is the deistic language of the Enlightenment.

This is made abundantly clear by the doctrine of the truth of all things: For the great teachers of a still-united Christian world it meant the indwelling of creation in God and of God

[64] On Sept. 16, 1785. Cf. Herder's other letter to Jacobi, on Feb. 6, 1784, in Herder, *Briefe*.

[65] Goethe, "Prooernion", Part II, in *Goethe the Lyrist; 100 Poems in Translation*, ed. Edwin H. Zeydel (Columbia: University of South Carolina Press, 1955), 167.

[66] *ST* I, 8, 3 ad 3.

[67] "Opportet quod Deus sit in omnibus rebus et intime." *ST* I, 8, 1.

in creation; for the philosophers of the Enlightenment, however, it had become the platitude that things are real because they belong, not to a dream, but—of course—to reality.

Chapter Three

I

The doctrine of the truth of all things does not have a theological meaning only. On the one hand, Thomas Aquinas writes: "All things are called true because of their orientation toward the truth of God's mind rather than (*principalius*) their orientation toward the truth of the human mind";[1] for "their relation to God's mind has priority over their relation to the human mind."[2] Nevertheless, this neither contradicts nor lessens his other statements: "Reality is called true in relation to the divine *and* the human mind."[3] And: "All things in nature are constituted in relation to two minds", the divine and the human mind, "and are called true as they conform to either the one or the other".[4]

How, then, are the two aspects here, the theological and the anthropological, tied together? How are they related one to the other? In the writings of Thomas Aquinas, this question is answered in two steps. The first step can be summed up as follows: The intrinsic nature of an object, its "form", mirrors its eternal archetype subsisting in the divine creative power; the forms of all things are in God as "Ideas". This is the direct and first meaning expressed in the principle of the truth of all things. "Because of its intrinsic form", which is patterned after the Idea in God, "an object can also essentially conform to our own perceiving mind."[5] "It is precisely through its intrin-

---

[1] "Res aliqua principalius dicitur vera in ordine ad veritatem intellectus divini quam in ordine ad veritatem intellectus humani." *Ver.* 1, 4.

[2] "Prior est comparatio ad intellectum divinum quam humanum." *Ver.* 1, 2.

[3] "Res autem dicitur vera per comparationem ad intellectum divinum et humanun." *Ver.* 1, 6.

[4] "Res ergo naturalis inter duos intellectus constituta, secundum adaequationem ad utrumque vera dicitur." *Ver.* 1, 2.

[5] "Res enim ipsa specie quam habet, divino intellectui adaequatur, sicut artificialis arti; et ex virtute ejusdem speciei nata est sibi intellectum nostrum adaequare." *Ver.* 1, 5 ad 2.

sic form that a thing mirrors the artistry of God's knowing mind, and at the same time proclaims within the [human] soul its own existence."[6] The truth of a thing consists in its correlation to a knowing mind; yet a thing is correlated to our human mind only because of its primary correlation to God's mind, a correlation that is actualized in the form of that thing. "All created things are constituted in relation to two minds":[7] "The things of nature, from which our mind receives its knowledge, are the measure for our mind; they themselves, in turn, receive their measure from God's knowing mind."[8] This means: the truth inherent in all things in view of God's mind is the foundation and root of their truth in view of the knowing human mind.

What specifically characterizes this truth of all things "in view of the human mind"? How is it distinct from the truth of all things "in view of God's mind"?

This leads us to the second step in the answer to the initial question. "All things without exception are known; actually known in God's mind, potentially known in the human mind. . . . Thus, the definition of a 'true object' can proclaim this object's actual perception by God's mind, but only its potential perception by a human mind."[9] "Truth is predicated of all things insofar as they actually conform to God's knowledge, or else, as they potentially are able to conform to human knowledge."[10] The truth of all things consists in their being known by God and being knowable by man; all things are

---

[6] "Ex hoc enim quod res formam habet, artem divini intellectus imitatur et sui notitiam in anima gignit." *Ver.* 1, 1 ad 3 contr. "Res autem extra animam per formam suam imitatur artem divini intellectus, et per eamdem nata est facere de se veram apprehensionem in intellectu humano, per quam etiam formam unaquaeque res esse habet." *Ver.* 1, 8. Cf. Kremer, "Synthèse", 334.

[7] *Ver.* 1, 2.

[8] "Res naturales, ex quibus intellectus noster scientiam accipit, mensurant intellectum nostrum . . . sed sunt mensuratae ab intellectu divino." *Ver.* 1, 2.

[9] "In definitione rei verae potest poni visio in actu intellectus divini, non autem visio intellectus humani, nisi in potentia." *Ver.* 1, 2 ad 4.

[10] "Verum . . . dicitur . . . de rebus secundum quod adaequantur intellectui divino vel aptae natae sunt adaequari intellectui humano." *Ver.* 1, 3.

knowable for man, however, only *because* they are already known by God. The lucidity which from the creative knowledge of the divine *Logos* flows into things, together with their very being—yes, even *as* their very being[11]—this lucidity alone makes all things knowable for the human mind. "The reality of a thing, in a way, is itself its light", as Thomas Aquinas says in a succinct and profound statement found in one of his last works.[12] This statement, indeed, reflects the Aristotelian doctrine that all things are knowable inasmuch as they are real[13] and also Plato's mystical wisdom of the "primordial light illuminating all that is".[14] We further see a conceptual connection here with a line found in Goethe's prose, declaring that "all facts are already their own theory", and "the phenomena in themselves are already the doctrine".[15]

Still, these lines of reflection, as they somehow direct our gaze toward the misty expanses of infinity, should not make us lose sight of the immediate subject matter at hand. Rather, we shall now pursue more specifically and directly our inquiry into the anthropological dimension implied in the principle of the truth of all things, and "corner that question" (as Goethe, again, was wont to say).[16]

In view of human cognition, "all things are true" means precisely that they stand revealed, open, intelligible—by reason of the primordial light emanating from the *Logos*, by reason of God's creative knowledge. "*Truth* adds to *being* the notion of *intelligibility*."[17]

This concept—that reality is accessible and intelligible—still needs to be more accurately described, defined and fathomed.

[11] "Quantum unumquodque habet de esse, tantum habet de intelligibilitate." *ST* I, 16, 1.

[12] "Ipsa actualitas rei est quoddam lumen ipsius." *Caus.* 1, 6. Thomas wrote the Commentary on the *Liber de causis* within the last five years of his life.

[13] Aristotle, *Metaphysics* 9, 9, 1051a.

[14] Plato, *Republic* 7, 540a.

[15] Goethe, *Maximen*, no. 993.

[16] Goethe, "Tag—und Jahreshefte", *Autobiographische Schriften* 3:474.

[17] "Verum enim addit supra ens rationem cognoscibilis." *De natura generis* 2.

2

What we have said so far will have made one thing clear: that things are knowable by the human mind is connected with their being known by God's creative mind, so intimately that their "truth" in view of human knowability has to be of the same kind, though analogous, as their primary "truth" in view of God's creative knowledge. Consequently, all reality, as reality, will essentially be intelligible for the human mind; and this intelligibility will be so inherent in reality's very being that "to be" and "to be intelligible for the human mind" become equivalent expressions. Everything that exists, therefore, can and must be judged accessible and intelligible for the searching human mind.

The first article of the *Quaestiones disputatae de veritate* by Thomas Aquinas contains of all his texts the most explicit and elaborate discussion of the *veritas rerum* [the truth of all things] as a "transcendental" concept. There, Thomas considers exclusively the orientation of all existing things toward the *anima*, the soul, and thus toward the *human* mind; the orientation toward God's creative knowledge is not even mentioned in this article.

The affirmation that all things are "open" and thus knowable for the human mind still needs to be safeguarded against possible misconceptions. "Truth predicated of things in view of human intellection pertains to them somehow accidentally. Just suppose the human mind did not and could not exist; even then would all things remain real and the same. Truth predicated of things, however, in view of God's intellection, belongs to them in absolute essence; they could not subsist without God 'knowing' and thus creating them."[18]

---

[18] "Veritas autem, quae dicitur de rebus in comparatione ad intellectum humanum, est rebus quodammodo accidentalis, quia posito quod intellectus humanus non esset nec esse posset, adhuc res in sua essentia permanerent. Sed veritas, quae dicitur de eis in comparatione ad intellectum divinum, eis inseparabiliter communicatur: non enim subsistere possunt nisi per intellectum divinum eas esse producentem." *Ver.* 1, 4.

How can this be reconciled with the previous affirmation that "knowable for the human mind" would be as essential to all things as their very being? Does not Thomas Aquinas, in speaking now of human truth as "somehow accidental", preclude the possibility, even necessity, of interpreting the "truth of all things", said to be interchangeable with their very being, as their openness also to human intellection? Not at all.

The knowability of all things by man is *secondary* to their being known by God. This, indeed, has to be stated with the utmost emphasis. That all things are essentially knowable constitutes the *second* meaning of their truth, not the *first*. Moreover, "the first meaning of truth is more intrinsic to things than the second; for their relationship to God's mind takes priority over their relationship to the human mind. Therefore, even in the absence of any human mind, things would still be called true, namely in view of God's knowing mind."[19] Still, the "second" meaning of the truth of all things, though secondary, is no less valid than the "first"; truth in this "second" sense pertains to all things in as real a way as the "first".

What, then, is Thomas Aquinas saying with his statement that truth predicated of things in view of human intellection pertains to them "somehow accidentally"? Simply this: being knowable, even being known, by a *human* mind is not constitutive of an object's essence; being known or not being known by *God*, however, means to be or not to be. Thomas is merely saying that only God's knowledge is creative in an absolute sense, and man's is not; that the intrinsic being of things is not affected, neither increased nor diminished, by man's eye gazing on them or not (while things exist because God sees them — according to Augustine!); that on the contrary the truth of all things relates to human intellection "as to its [the truth's]

[19] "Prima autem ratio veritatis per prius inest rei quam secunda, quia prior est comparatio ad intellectum divinum quam humanum; unde etiam si intellectus humanus non esset, adhuc res dicerentur verae in ordine ad intellectum divinum." *Ver.* 1, 2.

effect, insofar as the perceiving mind gains its knowledge
from these things".[20] In no wise does he say or imply that the
truth of all things in its "second" sense, related to the human
mind, would only be something extrinsic to things.[21]

Rather, the inner "light" that God's creative knowledge
confers on all things, thereby making them accessible to human perception, pertains to them as intrinsically as their very
being. All that exists is essentially open to human perception.
The form of things, their intrinsic configuration, is in its essence oriented toward becoming the possession of the human
mind (since "to know an object" means "to have its form").
"An object, by the very fact that it is real, is automatically
ready to conform to the perceiving mind"[22] "and therefore is
called here 'true' ".[23] "There are many things that our mind
actually does not know; and yet, there is nothing . . . that the
human mind could not perceive, at least potentially."[24]

---

[20] "(Veritas rei comparatur) ad humanum (intellectum) quodammodo
quasi ad effectum, in quantum intellectus a rebus scientiam accepit." *Ver.* 1,
4.

[21] Sertillanges, *Thomas*, 69: "We know, of course, that the relation of all
things to us is not part of their inner nature. Thomas' philosophy ascribes to
things their own autonomy and considers it accidental to their inner being
whether they are known by us or not. Nonetheless, considering the idea-
based relations of things to us, we may maintain that a thing is true insofar
as it corresponds to the concept that we have of it." This opinion, I propose,
is not in agreement with Thomas Aquinas' conception of truth. First: Thomas
considers truth to belong to the intrinsic nature of things; has he not, in *Ver.*
1, 1, developed the concept of transcendental 'truth' as being interchangeable
with the concept of 'being', and this precisely in reference to the *human mind*?
Second: Thomas calls things true, not because they "correspond to the concept we have of them", but because they allow our mind to gain a true concept of them. It is therefore the other way around: concepts are true inasmuch
as they correspond to the respective objects.

[22] "Ex hoc quod aliquid habet de entitate, secundum hoc natum est aequari
intellectui." *Ver.* 1, 1 ad 5.

[23] "Secundum hoc quod habet aliquid de entitate, natum est conformari intellectui, et secundum hoc consequitur ibi ratio veri." *Ver.* 1, 1 ad 2 contr.

[24] "Sunt enim multae res, quae intellectu nostro non cognoscuntur; nulla
tamen res est, quam intellectus divinus actu non cognoscat et intellectus humanus in potentia." *Ver.* 1, 2 ad 4.

3

This last statement cautions against taking the "second" meaning of the truth of all things, their intelligibility, in too literal a sense. "Intelligibility" as the all-encompassing trait of everything that exists, does not mean that all reality, indiscriminately, could readily be grasped and comprehended by the human mind.

Rather, the moment we accept *ens* and *verum*—that is, *being* and *being intelligible*—to be interchangeable, there appears a surprising consequence. For in that case an object would indeed be all the more intelligible, the higher it ranks in the order of being. And, consequently, the highest form of being would have to be true and intelligible in the highest sense. In reality, however, the highest level of being is least accessible and least comprehensible for our mind, and the reality of God remains totally beyond human understanding. We are faced with this conclusion: the more an object is true and therefore knowable in itself, the less it is comprehensible for the human mind.

This somewhat strange and dissonant conclusion appears in the writings of Thomas Aquinas many times and in explicit terms, a surprise only to those who mistook for the historic original the distorted picture of Thomas painted by the Wolffian Enlightenment. Thomas frequently quotes with unreserved approval the statement from Aristotle's *Metaphysics* that considers our soul's perceptive powers regarding what is clearest in itself and compares those powers to the eyes of nocturnal birds regarding the light of day.[25] And in the *Quaestiones disputatae de veritate* we even read: "The less perspicuous a thing is in itself, the more perspicuous it appears in relation to us."[26]

---

[25] Aristotle, *Metaphysics* 2, 1, 993b. Cf. *CG* 3, 25.
[26] "Ea quae sunt minus nota in se, nota sunt magis quoad nos." *Ver.* 10, 12 ad 6.

Still, even those created things that are most perspicuous in relation to us we can never comprehend fully. To comprehend, indeed, means: to know an object as much as it is knowable in itself, to transform all potential knowledge into actual knowledge, to exhaust every possibility of knowing more.[27] But a finite mind is never capable of grasping all the potential knowledge offered by any existing reality. Rather, whatever is knowable in and of an object itself, always and necessarily exceeds what can actually be known.

> Like ever flowing, ever full a well:
> The world knows more than mortal man can tell.[28]

Are we now forced to draw this contradictory conclusion: the clearer a thing, the more shrouded it is; the darker a thing, the more knowable it is? By no means!

If some reality remains hidden to our perception, the reason could logically be either our own cognitive shortcoming or the objective darkness of that reality.[29] (Such a hypothesis, strictly speaking, is already illusory: the truth of all things, their lucidity, is a primordial reality not even open to "methodical" abstraction.) Thomas Aquinas states: our cognitive difficulties do not result from some objective darkness in an object but rather from "our inadequate perceptive powers".[30] All things are intrinsically knowable, including those realms that remain hidden to us. The water in the well of meaning, even after the most eager draught, remains "ever flowing, ever full", ready to quench the searing thirst of our deeper quest. Reality ultimately remains incomprehensible, not be-

---

[27] Joh. 1, 11.
[28] "Ein Wasser, das sich ewig trinkt und hält: / So unbegreiflich ist der Sinn der Welt." Konrad Weiss, Gedichte (München, 1961), 672.
[29] "Sic igitur potest contingere quod veritas sit difficilis ad cognoscendum, vel propter defectum qui est in ipsis rebus, vel propter defectum qui est in intellectu nostro." Met. 2, 1, no. 279.
[30] "Difficultas accidit in cognitione veritatis maxime propter defectum intellectus nostri." Met. 2, 1, no. 282. "Non tamen principalis causa difficultatis est ex parte rerum, sed ex parte nostra." Met. 2, 1, no. 281.

cause of any intrinsic darkness, but because its lucidity is unfathomable. In this we also find what distinguishes the created
things in nature from the works of man: the former are unfathomable and "ever full", whereas the latter soon run dry
and leave us with the taste of bitter dregs. And the greater a
human work, the more it compares to the natural things in
God's creation, which also reveal to the perceiving mind ever
deeper levels of still unexplored knowledge.

For Thomas Aquinas all things are intrinsically lucid and intelligible, even though our own perceptive powers will never
grasp them fully. In his commentary on Aristotle's *Metaphysics* he concludes the comparison between the most obvious realities and the eyes of nocturnal birds with these striking
words: "Though the eye of the night owl may not see the sun,
the eye of the eagle still gazes on it."[31]

4

All things, then, are knowable in themselves. All that exists,
because it exists, is ordered toward a knowing mind, even toward the finite human mind. This means: not only is the eye
sun-related, the sun as well is eye-related; all that has being is
mind-related in its most intrinsic core. Mind and being are interconnected.

There exists an absolute objectivism, advanced at times, not
surprisingly, by none other than the Kantianism of the Marburg school. This objectivism, in relation to the teaching of
the truth of all things, most strikingly resembles the deism of
the Enlightenment. Such deism puts God outside this world
in a distorted sense and so dissolves and destroys the "first"
meaning of the truth of all things, which sees all things contained in God's creative knowledge and the eternal archetypes
contained in all things. In the same way does an absolute objectivism cancel the "second" meaning of the truth of all

[31] "Solem etsi non videat oculus nycticoracis, videt tamen eum oculus aq-
uilae." *Met.* 2, 1, no. 286. Cf. Pieper, *Licht*, 13ff.

things by insisting that all existing reality is radically self-contained and independent, especially in relation to the perceiving human mind.[32]

The complex and profound study on the "Problems of the Immaterial" by Nicolai Hartmann, for example, offers the following statements: "No existing thing, as of itself, is an object. . . . Whether it becomes an object or not does not depend on the thing itself but on the ability of a mind to make it its object."[33] "The subject-object relationship is a specific creation on the part of the mind. It would not exist in the world without the mind; it comes into the world through the mind."[34] Such "objectivation" happens when "a consciousness constitutes itself the subject of an object",[35] and with this a thing "enters a relationship to man, a relationship otherwise not present in any thing. . . . A thing's being of itself is not 'ordered toward' anyone."[36]

Nicolai Hartmann's book, without doubt one of the major philosophical statements of our time, has been interpreted, strangely enough, as being rooted in the tenets of traditional ontology.[37] Such an interpretation, however, misses the mark entirely.

We would go beyond the confines of this inquiry, which aims primarily at exposition, were we to argue with Nicolai Hartmann's position or with the erroneous way it has been understood. Still, we might benefit if we once again state the

---

[32] "Entre l'être et l'esprit il n'y a pas, dans la synthèse thomiste, cette relation de totale indépendance ou cette absence de relation que certains philosophes contemporains ont imaginée pour sauver la réalité de l'object." Kremer, "Synthèse", 331.

[33] Hartmann, *Problem des geistigen Seins*, 101.

[34] Hartmann, *Problem des geistigen Seins*, 104.

[35] Hartmann, *Problem des geistigen Seins*, 104.

[36] Hartmann, *Problem des geistigen Seins*, 106.

[37] Getzeny, *Vom Wesen zum Sein*, 62: "Nicolai Hartmann, in his uncompromising affirmation of *being* and its independence from thought, stands squarely in the line of the great tradition of Christian philosophy. This is demonstrated by the decisive connection he establishes back to Aristotle above all, but also to the Scholastics, to Leibniz, and to Christian Wolff."

"second" meaning of the truth of all things as formulated in the ontological systems of the High Middle Ages, comparing and contrasting it with Hartmann's thesis. Pointing out the differences here will even more clearly define the principle of the truth of all things.

There are mainly two differences. The first: the principle of the truth of all things affirms that all things, in fact, are "objects" in and of themselves, that they indeed are intrinsically "oriented toward someone".[38] Truth, understood as knowability, is inherent in all things together with their very being. There is absolutely no alternative possibility, as if a thing may or may not be intelligible for man, the way a game animal may or may not become the prey of a hunter. Rather, it is part of a thing's essence to be intelligible; that is, to be ordered, by itself, toward a knowing mind, including the finite mind. "By itself"—this means: by God. It is not of the essence of a thing to be *actually* perceived by a finite mind; it is of its essence, however, to be *potentially* perceived. In no wise does an objective reality perdure in total and unrelated isolation "unto itself" unless and until our mind would make it its object. "To be true" means the same as "to manifest and reveal being".[39] "The truth of a thing is what reveals its essence."[40] This quality of manifesting, revealing, showing is intrinsic to all things as such, so that it is these things themselves that reveal and show what they are; it is their very being that makes them manifest themselves. (One might remember here Spinoza who saw all things as "mute".) Manifesting, revealing, proclaiming—all these terms indicate orientation toward a listener, a recipient, a person.

---

[38] "The concept of *verum* stands for being, insofar as such being is the object of a mind. It means the aspect of being that constitutes the target or the object of a perceiving subject." Söhngen, *Sein und Gegenstand*, 115.

[39] "Verum est manifestativum et declarativum esse." *Ver.* 1, 1 (quotation from Hilary).

[40] "Veritas est qua ostenditur id quod est." Augustine, *De vera religione*, chap. 36; quoted in *Ver.* 1, 1.

The second difference: our perceiving mind, in directing its attention toward an object, does not at all establish only then a correlation with that object. Rather, a mutual correlation between *being* and *mind* exists already prior to any actual perception. The object-subject relationship, in traditional ontology, is not at all "a creation on the part of the mind", as Nicolai Hartmann would have it; it precedes any activity of the mind. It is therefore incorrect to say that "a consciousness constitutes itself the subject of an object"; not through its own decision is the finite mind a subject, the master of its own interrelation with reality. Reality in itself is oriented toward man's perceiving mind, without the mind's contribution, and simply by virtue of its very *being*, which man has not bestowed on it. Moreover, the human mind in turn is ordered toward the realm of existing things, also not by its own doing but by virtue of its very *being*, which, again, is not its own creation. This orientation of the human mind toward reality precedes any of the mind's own choices and decisions. A finite mind is in its essence geared toward the knowledge of reality—"In its essence" meaning: by force by intrinsic, inescapable necessity.[41]

It is specifically this mutual and antecedent correlation between objective reality and subjective cognition that Goethe had in mind when he spoke of the "synthesis of world and mind, which provides the most blessed assurance about the eternal harmony of the universe".[42] And among Novalis' philosophical propositions we find this one: "Wherever there is being, there also must be cognition."[43]

Thomas Aquinas, indeed, took the teaching that the intrinsic correlation between mind and reality always precedes any actual cognition; he summed it up, once again in such a way as to turn our normal manner of thinking inside out, as it were. The formulation appears in the first article of the *Quaes-*

[41] "Intellectus . . . naturaliter appetit intelligibile ut est intelligible; appetit enim naturaliter intellectus intelligere." *An.* 13 ad 11.

[42] Goether, *Maximen*, no. 1164.

[43] Novalis, *Werke und Briefe* (Leipzig, 1942), 409.

tiones disputatae de veritate, a chapter abundantly rich in thought and in this study quoted repeatedly. There we read: "Our knowledge, in a certain sense, is the offspring of truth."[44]

---

[44] "Cognitio est quidam veritatis effectus." *Ver.* 1, 1. "If our mind were not by its nature already in touch with reality, it would never be able to reach reality at all." Rohner, "Grundproblem", 1087.

Chapter Four

Although the preceding chapters should have made quite clear the concept of the truth of all things as related to human perception, the inquiry itself into the specifically anthropological meaning of that principle still remains incomplete. We have not yet answered the question why that principle should enlighten or at all affect our conception of man. To describe just this will be the final and fundamental task here. First, however, some historical remarks are in order.

Wherever we find ontological reflections, from the early Greek classics to the German Enlightenment, we also find elements and aspects of the teaching on the truth of all things. Still, the full and complete concept of the truth of all that exists, uniting in one harmonious structure the many different elements, is nowhere to be found, except in the writings of Thomas Aquinas.

Our study already mentioned repeatedly the *Aristotelian* and *Platonic* roots, which in turn derive from even more ancient origins. Indeed, within the realm of Western ontology and metaphysics we may not easily discover any major idea that would not in some way point back to those two great philosophers. We have met *Augustine* as well, who shortly will tell us more.

Thomas himself, in addition to quoting these three, especially uses the important Arab philosophers of the early Middle Ages, Avicenna and Averroes. *Avicenna* (980–1037) has been called the "interpreter of Greek thinking for the Orient".[1] In his voluminous *Book of Healing for the Soul* we read, for instance, that the things of this world "are nothing but God's knowledge"; "as God conceives a thing, it comes into existence; it becomes reality only because it has been con-

---

[1] Überweg, *Geschichte* 2:307.

ceived as idea."² Avicenna's formal definition of the truth of
all things is quoted by Thomas repeatedly;³ more on this
shortly. The *Brief Commentary* on Aristotle's *Metaphysics* by
Averroës (1126–98), of overwhelming importance for the history of Western philosophy, speaks—perhaps for the first
time—of all things as by their very nature intelligible for the
human mind because their being springs from the artistry of
a creator's mind.⁴ The core of this idea, though, had found an
even more precise formulation a century earlier in *Anselm of
Canterbury's* (1033–1109) *Dialogue on Truth*, which places particular emphasis on the truth inherent in all things—witness
the motto prefacing our study. In the tenth chapter of this *Dialogue* we read: "Thus is the truth inherent in the being of all
things indeed the effect of the highest Truth, and at the same
time the cause of the other truth that pertains to human cognition." *Alexander of Hales* (ca. 1170–1245) was the first in the
West to draw attention to Aristotle's *Metaphysics* and its Arab
commentators. Yet his own conception of the truth of all
things is much more influenced by Augustine. Alexander of
Hales understands this concept, on the one hand, as the conformity of a thing with its archetypical idea in God⁵ and also
as the specific quality that renders an object intelligible.⁶ On

² Avicenna, *Metaphysik* 8, 7 (Horten, p. 533).

³ *CG* I, 60; *Ver.* I, 2; *ST* I, 16, 1.

⁴ The things of this world "are oriented in their inner nature toward being
known by us: for this knowability is an essential determination and belongs
to their real nature. . . ." Those things fashioned through artistry "are con-
ceptually [spiritually] perceived by someone who has not made them. . . .
They constitute a basis for this 'spiritual dimension' [i.e., their knowability]
only because they originate from a spiritual principle [the mind of the artist]."
Averroes, *Metaphysik* (Horten, 60f.).

⁵ "He in turn relates this triad, *unum, verum, bonum,* back to the threefold
conformity of all things with God as *causa efficiens, exemplaris* and *finalis.* It is
also from the one God that all the different manifestations derive their unity;
the truth of all that is rests on the exemplary Ideas in God, and toward him, the
highest good, are all things oriented in a purposeful manner, since he is their
ultimate end." Schulemann, *Transzendentalien*, 26f.

⁶ "Verum enim est, quo res habet discerni." Alexander of Hales, *Summa
theologica*, I, 13, 1; quoted from Knittermeyer, *Terminus*, 21.

the other hand, he gives this concept's meaning as "the undivided inner unity of being and all that is".[7] This latter thought is also expressed in Avicenna's writings, which Alexander knew especially well and quoted frequently.[8] Still, as a Franciscan beholden to Augustine, Alexander may have included this definition in his *Summa* because it was eminently legitimated by its occurrence in Augustine's work.

Augustine, in fact, had stated: *Verum mihi videtur id quod est*; "truth, it seems to me, is that which *is*."[9] Considering only what is stated explicitly, we see here the truth of things defined as reality's intrinsic orientation toward nothing but itself, as *being's* identity with itself. However, Augustine himself, and also his followers, never interpreted this as an affirmation of independence from God's creative knowledge.[10] Still, the ambiguous formulation, "truth is that which *is*", apparently started a development that left the original concept of truth progressively more narrow and more shallow. The Enlightenment's idea of truth, polemicized by Kant as stating, "truth means: each thing is what it is"[11]—this entirely degenerated concept can claim the same lineage as well.

Thomas Aquinas explicitly maintains that Augustine's definition fails to capture the total meaning of truth.[12] Missing in it is precisely the most important and truly essential element: the orientation toward the knowing mind.[13] It is not reality's

[7] "Veritas est indivisio esse et ejus quod est." Alexander of Hales, *Summa theologica*, I, 1, 3, 2, 2.

[8] Überweg, *Geschichte* 2:384.

[9] Augustine, *Soliloquia*, 2, 5.

[10] Cf. Augustine, *Confessions*, 13, 38. "It was, incidentally, Albertus Magnus who maintained that Augustine was the first to consider *unum, verum, bonum* as a *vestigium trinitatis* (commentary on the *Liber Sententiarum* 1, d. 3, art. 15)." Knittermeyer, *Terminus,* 32f.

[11] Erdmann, "Mitteilungen", 81.

[12] "Ista definitio 'verum est id quod est' non perfecte exprimit rationem veritatis, sed quasi matrialiter tantum." *Ver.* 1, 10 ad 1.

[13] "La vérité n'est pas un pur synonyme de l'être, qu'elle n'indique pas l'être simplement conçu comme tel, mais comme en relation avec l'intelligence. Ce point de vue n'est peut-être pas suffisamment expliqué par les Augustiniens." Domet de Vorges, *Abrégé* 1:107.

identity with itself that establishes its truth, but its (actual or potential) identity with the knowing mind. Avicenna's conception of truth, as mentioned earlier, is comparable to Augustine's. In a compendium of his *Metaphysics* we read: "The truth of each thing is its specific manner of being, which is its enduring proper nature."[14] Thomas Aquinas quotes this and Augustine's definition several times, occasionally in such a way as to give the impression that he would subscribe to it entirely. In the *Summa contra Gentiles*, for example, he states: a thing is called "true" insofar as it reaches the actualization of its proper essence; "for this reason Avicenna says in his *Metaphysics* . . ."—and the above-mentioned definition follows. But then Thomas immediately adds a clarification that is rather a reinterpretation and correction than an explanation: ". . . but only insofar as such a thing is by its nature designed to produce a true perception of itself, and insofar as it conforms to its proper idea that resides in God's mind".[15] Into Avicenna's conception of truth Thomas evidently injects here the orientation toward the divine as well as the human mind. And in a different place he cites Augustine's and also Avicenna's definition of truth in support of his own position: reality is called "true as it conforms to God's knowing mind, and insofar as it actualizes the ideal toward which it is ordered by God's knowing mind".[16] Although we should not deny the deeper historical justification for such reinterpretations, we must nevertheless not brush aside the original differences.

[14] "Cujuscumque enim rei veritas est proprietas sui esse quod stabilitur ei." Avicenna, *Compendium* 1, 2, 1, 8. This is how Thomas quotes the same passage: "Veritas rei est proprietas esse uniuscujusque rei, quod stabilitum est ei." *CG* 1, 60.
[15] "Res . . . vera dicitur, secundum quod actum propriae naturae consequitur; unde Avicenna dicit in sua Metaphysica, quod 'veritas rei est proprietas esse uniuscujusque rei, quod stabilitum est ei', inquantum talis res nata est de se facere veram aestimationem et inquantum propriam sui rationem, quae est in mente divina, imitatur." *CG* 1, 60.
[16] *Ver.* 1, 2.

Albertus Magnus generally follows Augustine's and Avicenna's lead in defining the truth of all things. This will surprise only those who see Albertus exclusively as the one who prepared the way for the Aristotelian renaissance. It is, however, no less important to realize that he had read his teacher Aristotle mainly through the eyes of the commentator Avicenna[17] and that the Augustinian (as well as the Platonic and Neoplatonic) tradition exerted a decisive influence in this great German's work. Albertus Magnus, then, defines the truth of a thing as correspondence to its proper essential form.[18] Because the essential form makes a thing what it is, his definition means: truth is the identity of a thing with itself. We should once again point out that Albertus' way of conceiving the "form" of a thing is not excluding a correlation to God's creative knowledge.[19] Still, the explicit formulation is open to the same misinterpretation Augustine's definition has prompted. Like the latter, so also is Albertus' conception of truth unmistakably different from that of Thomas Aquinas. At any rate, to declare the much greater disciple dependent in this point on his teacher, as claimed in a new "historico-systematic" study, is utterly unjustified.[20]

---

[17] Überweg, *Geschichte* 2:409.

[18] "Verum convertitur cum ente secundum supposita et addit supra intentionem entis relationem ad actum qui est forma." Albertus, *Summa de bono* 1, 4, 1. "Verum enim semper addit supra ens relationem ad forman sive ad id, quo est res formaliter." Albertus, *Summa de bono* 1, 4, 3. Cf. Kühle, "Lehre", 139.

[19] Albertus saw the concepts of *unum, verum, bonum* primarily actualized in God. Cf. Schulemann, *Transzendentalien*, 27.

[20] "Albertus conceives the *verum* as the identity of a being with its intrinsic form. Thus, the notions of *actual being* and *verum* become equivalent. Thomas' thinking moves with the same ontological context. He, too, declares a thing true insofar as it possesses the essential form of its nature, and so is identical with the substance of its being. But for him the concept of truth is so closely related to the mind that his fundamental interpretation of *verum* cannot do without the notion of conformity to the mind." Hans Meyer, *Thomas von Aquin*, 162. This is quite imprecise, also grammatically, and will not bear closer scrutiny.

After all, it is simply impossible to explain in terms of "influences" and "predecessors" the immense methodical power with which Thomas Aquinas seized the available and as yet unformed body of thought, absorbed it into the ordering structure of his intellect and molded it into his own unified, original system. Although Thomas clearly considered himself embedded in a larger intellectual tradition, still his methodical power shines forth fresh and young and unique as all that truly is of genius.

2

It is not our intention to trace the concept of truth and its definition from Thomas' time up to our own era. Still, some representative thinkers, including Duns Scotus and Francisco Suarez, should be considered briefly. It may further be of interest to identify more specifically the sources from which derived the Enlightenment's concept of the truth of all things.

Duns Scotus (1266–1308), rightly considered an opponent of Thomas Aquinas, nevertheless, and surprisingly so, follows the latter closely. Duns Scotus, too, sees the truth of all things first of all as their knowability: "Truth, of which the Philosopher [Aristotle, *II Metaph.*] says, 'as reality relates to being, so also to truth', must be understood as the inner openness of all things in themselves, or as their knowability based on what each of them specifically is."[21] "Inasmuch as a thing has being, so also is it essentially ordered to be known in truth."[22] The

[21] "Et ita debet intelligi veritas, de qua loquitur Philosophus II. Metaph., 'Sicut res se habent ad entitatem, ita ad veritatem', pro evidentia rei in se sive pro intelligibilitate rei ex parte sui." Duns Scotus *Oxoniensia* 1, d. 3, 1 et 2, 7, no. 364.

[22] "Sequitur quod unumquodque eo modo, quo habet esse, habeat etiam veritatem. . . . Sicut res habet esse, sic etiam est apta nata vere cognosci." Duns Scotus, *In Met.* 2, Summa I, cap. 2, no. 8. "Est enim veritas in rebus et veritas in intellectu. In rebus dupliciter, in genere, videlicet per comparationem ad producentem et per comparationem ad cognoscentem sive intelligentem. Primo modo dicitur veritas absolute conformitas producti ad

actual fact of being known, however, taken as an intrinsic property of *being* as such, pertains to all existing things only if referred to God's knowledge. Only in view of God's knowledge can we comprehend the definition, "truth is the conformity of an object to its idea."[23] The same concept of the truth of all things apparently perdured all through the later Scotism as well.[24]

The great Spanish Scholastic *Francisco Suarez* (1548–1617) has also been depicted above all as being in opposition to Thomas Aquinas.[25] And we recall how Christian Wolff declared his own conception of truth to coincide in fact with the position of Suarez.[26] We should indeed admit that Suarez appears to have eliminated the concepts of *res* and *aliquid* from the realm

---

producens. . . . Secundo modo, scilicet per comparationem ad intellectum, dicitur res vera tripliciter. Primo, quia sui manifestativa, quantum est de se, cuicumque intellectui potenti manifestationem cognoscere." Duns Scotus *In Met.* 6, qu. 3, no. 5.

[23] "Non opportet autem quod res sicut se habet ad entitatem, sic se habeat ad cognisci, nisi intelligatur cognosci ab illo intellectu, qui respicit intelligibilia omnia secundum gradum proprium cognoscibilitatis eorum, qualis non est noster intellectus." Duns Scotus *Oxoniensia* 1, d. 3, 1 et 2, 7, no. 364; similarly also *Oxoniensia* 1, d. 3, 3, 5, no. 395. "Veritas est conformitas exemplaris ad exemplata." Duns Scotus *Collationes* 19, 1.

[24] Cf. Garcia's Scotistic *Lexicon*, s.v. "veritas".

[25] So Eschweiler, "Spanische Spätscholastik", 275ff. He mentions "the common opinion that accepts the Jesuits' academic philosophy of the early seventeenth century, then dominant in Europe, as 'basically true' to Thomas", and labels this opinion "unjustified and superficial" (p. 282). Max Wundt, *Schulmetaphysik*, 268ff., has discussed this thesis extensively. Regarding the alleged differences between Thomas and Suarez, he says: "Eschweiler's quotations, on closer scrutiny, make it doubtful that they actually prove the point." Wundt finds it "incomprehensible" that a "Catholic scholar indeed" should have so thoroughly misjudged the common ground between Thomas and Suarez, and he wonders "whether nowadays the differences between Thomas and Suarez are not overemphasized" (p. 270ff.). As we have shown in this study, there are no essential differences between Thomas Aquinas and Suarez regarding the doctrine of the truth of all things.

Klasmeier's dissertation on Suarez, *Transzendentalienlehre*, is incredibly imprecise in the quotation and interpretation of its original texts and therefore, sad to say, entirely useless.

[26] Wolff, *Philosophia prima*, paragraph 502. Cf. chap. 1, no. 3.

of the transcendentals, thus reducing the latter to three: *unum, verum,* and *bonum.*[27] Regarding the doctrine of the truth of all things, however, we cannot really speak of opposing positions between Thomas Aquinas and Suarez. Wolff's affirmation, therefore, has to be incorrect. Wolff maintains that Suarez holds things to be true "independent of a knowing mind", thus making "truth" a property of reality as such, even under the impossible assumption that this reality be related neither to the divine nor the human mind.[28] This position, of course, would contradict Thomas Aquinas, who holds the exact opposite: "Even without the human mind would reality still be called true—in relation to God's knowing mind. But should we assume the impossible, that there be neither the human nor the divine mind, then no basis at all would remain to speak of 'truth'."[29] This precisely is Suarez' position, too. The very passage from the *Disputationes Metaphysicae* quoted by Wolff contains these statements: "The fact that reality is intelligible also makes it true."[30] "All that exists is intrinsically ordered to conform to a knowing mind; indeed, there is nothing that would not actually conform at least to God's knowing mind."[31] And there is the statement itself on which Wolff seems to rely primarily: "Transcendental truth means the same as the *being* of a thing". Yet this statement, too, continues, "directly implying the knowledge or the concept residing in the mind to which

[27] Willmann, *Idealismus* 3:117.

[28] Wolff, *Philsophia prima*, paragraph 502.

[29] "Sed si uterque intellectus, quod est impossibile, intelligeretur auferri, nullo modo veritatis ratio remaneret." *Ver.* 1, 2.

[30] "Hoc ipso, quod ens est intelligible, verum est." Suarez, *Met. Disp.* 8, 7, no. 7.

[31] "Ex his intelligitur primo, quomodo esse verum conveniat omni enti reali, sive creato sive increato: quia omne ens de se est aptum conformari intellectui; immo nullum est ens, quod non sit actu conforme alicui intellectui, saltem divino." Suarez, *Met. Disp.* 8, 7, no. 35. Überweg, *Geschichte* 3:211ff., has this to say on Surarez' position regarding transcendentals: "Transcendental truth is the intelligibility of reality as an inseparable dimension of its intrinsic nature, and this in relation to the created mind as well as to the mind of God."

such a reality conforms, or in which it is actually or potentially represented in its true being."[32] We have already mentioned how Wolff's opinion of himself, as being in agreement with Scholasticism, was frequently accepted even in unlikely quarters. Thus Suarez' statement just quoted has occasionally been misunderstood in a sense similar to Wolff's interpretation also in Neoscholastic circles. Stöckl, for instance, in his extensive *Geschichte der Philosophie des Mittelalters* [History of Philosophy in the Middle Ages], asserts that Suarez' concept of the *verum* would "envision, but only *secondarily* and by connotation, *also* a relation toward a knowing mind."[33] Suarez himself, however, not unlike Thomas, sees in this same relationship the very essence of the truth of reality.[34]

Gabriel Vasquez (1551–1604), a contemporary and compatriot of Suarez', in his *Commentaria ac Disputationes* [Explanations and Discussions] of Thomas Aquinas' *Summa Theologica*, has also extensively dealt with the concept of the truth of all things—not, however, according to the mind of the *Summa's* author, whom he presumes to interpret. We should briefly consider his teaching because of its wider and lasting consequences, which certainly contributed to the decay of the original doctrine of the truth of all things. Vasquez paves the way for the subsequent, almost unanimous outright rejection of this concept. The term "truth", according to Vasquez, would apply to reality not in a direct and proper sense, but only by analogy, "in the way a medicine is called 'healthy' in view of the health it may effect in someone".[35] And the same view-

[32] "Veritas transcendentalis significat entitatem rei, connotando cognitionem seu conceptum intellectus, cui talis entitas conformatur, vel in quo talis res repraesentatur, vel repraesentari potest prout est." Suarez, *Met. Disp.* 8, 7, no. 25.

[33] Stöckl, *Geschichte* 3:647.

[34] Schulemann, *Transzendentalien*, 71, also seems to think of Wolff's position on transcendentals as representing the teachings of Suarez.

[35] Vasquez, *Commentaria* 77, 4. Cf. in contrast *Ver.* 1, 4 (conclusion) where the image of the "healthy" medicine is also employed, though in a different sense.

point, he says, was already advanced by Hervaeus, Durandus and Henricus. The latter two, Henry of Ghent (1217–93) and Durandus of Saint-Pourçain (ca. 1270–1334), known to their contemporaries as *Doctor solemnis* and *Doctor modernus*, respectively, both stand squarely in the Augustinian philosophical tradition—a significant aspect indeed. Otto Willmann had Durandus of Saint-Pourçain in mind when he remarked, as quoted previously, that "as the Ideas are thrown out, there also go the transcendentals".[36] What started here found its logical completion in the philosophy of the Enlightenment.

Max Wundt sees the *German Academic Metaphysicians* of the seventeenth century as "still trying to preserve the philosophical tradition undiminished, while the 'new' philosophers were interested only in certain aspects of the inherited body of teaching, developing those aspects one-sidedly and outside the original context".[37] It comes indeed as a total surprise to learn from Wundt's study that Thomas Aquinas, for example, was looked on as the obligatory authority even in the Protestant metaphysical circles of German universities; that there "he was considered the most important teacher of the Middle Ages, and best suited to do justice to any differences in doctrine. One would gladly accept standing under the shadow of his reputation."[38]

How then did these schoolmen of the seventeenth century see the concept of the truth of all things? They define it, in complete accordance with the traditional ontology, invariably as the orientation of all things toward the knowing mind. "Truth is the mode of being by which it conforms to the human and the divine mind, so that *truth* and *being* are interchangeable", as Bartholomäus Keckermann (1571–1609)

[36] Willmann, *Idealismus* 3:583.
[37] Wundt, *Schulmetaphysik*, 28.
[38] Wundt, *Schulmetaphysik*, 12. Wundt also reports that Michael Wolff, professor in Jena, republished Thomas Aquinas' *De ente et essentia* in 1618 and used it as the basis for his lectures (p. 37). And Cornelius Martini, in part two of his *Metaphysica commentatio*, recommended to those who desired more information also Thomas' treatise *De ente et essentia* (p. 101).

states.[39] Daniel Cramer (1568–1637), too, determines transcendental truth to be *conformitas rei ad intellectum* [conformity of object and mind]. Teaching in Wittenberg, he was the first Lutheran professor who—after a century of antimetaphysics—wrote again a treatise on metaphysics (1594).[40] Max Wundt—to refer once more to his book—mentions several other names, including Cornelius Martini, Jakob Martini and Abraham Calov.[41] Still, there are clear proponents as well of that other definition of truth, which says: the truth of all things consists in their identity with themselves. It is not surprising to hear the Cartesian philosopher, Johann Clauberg (1622–65), declare: "Since anything that exists conforms to its specific idea or definition (!), which indeed is nothing else but the representation and expression of its essence, it follows that all that is, is true."[42] But consider this statement, too: "The truth of all that exists lies in its conformity with the principles of its being", taken from the *Metaphysica* of the "Scholastic" Maccovius: such a formulation does not appear to be unusual in the seventeenth century, even in those philosophical works that are metaphysically oriented and substantially influenced by the traditional ontology.[43] Does that formulation not closely resemble the definition of a Wolff, a Baumgarten?

Still, the exact meaning of such statements within the academic philosophy of the seventeenth century no doubt differs

[39] Keckermann, *Metaphysicae brevissima synopsis et compendium*; quoted from Knittermeyer, *Terminus*, 124.

[40] Under the title, *Isagoge in Metaphysicam Aristotelis* (Hannover, 1594). Cf. Knittermeyer, *Terminus*, 115.

[41] Wundt, *Schulmetaphysik*, 189.

[42] "Quoniam res omnis cum sua idea sive definitione convenit, quippe quae nihil aliud est quam essentiae ejus repraesentatio et explicatio . . . patet omne ens esse verum." Clauberg, *Opera philosophica* (Amsterdam, 1691), 208; quoted from Knittermeyer, *Terminus*, 171.

[43] "Veritas rei est congruentia cum suis principiis." Maccovius, *Metaphysica* 1, 7; similarly: Burgersdijk *Institutiones metaphysicae* 1, 18, 9. The following statement, in Rudrauff *Institutiones et decisiones metaphysicae* 1, 1, 2, 2, points in the same direction: "Veritas entitativa est convenientia essentiae enti inesse debitae." All quoted from Wundt, *Schulmetaphysik*.

substantially from what the Enlightenment later tried to express in identical words. What those schoolmen really meant to say in their metaphysics is clearly expressed by Rudolf Goclenius (1547–1628), professor at Marburg University, in his once-celebrated *Lexicon philosophicum*, "a key to open up philosophy's doors", as its title promises. His definition of the truth of all things definitely harks back to Augustine, Avicenna and Alexander of Hales. Goclenius, like the reformed teachers in general,[44] was less beholden to Thomas Aquinas than, for instance, to his Lutheran contemporaries and colleagues. First he determines the truth of all things to consist in their "identity with themselves", but then immediately he refers to their original ideas in God, following in this, too, Augustine's position.

To show himself in agreement with the "Scholastics", Wolff quotes, in addition to Suarez' *Disputationes*, also Goclenius' *Lexicon philosophicum*.[45] Goclenius, in his own conception of truth, stands certainly closer to Christian Wolff than the true "Thomists", but to connect the one with the other still amounts to bridging an abyss. That Wolff fails or refuses to acknowledge this abyss only accentuates it. Thus, the difference between Wolff's and Goclenius' conception of the truth of all things illustrates as in a nutshell what has happened in "modern" philosophy: Goclenius defines "transcendental truth" as "conformity of all things with God's mind and with their own essence".[46] Wolff instead drops the first part of this definition; all that remains is the second part.

Kant then declared this shallow residue "sterile and tautological" and rightly eliminated it from philosophical discourse.

[44] Wundt, *Schulmetaphysik*, 12.

[45] Wolff, *Philosophia prima*, paragraph 502.

[46] "Veritas metaphysica: conformitas rei cum mente divina et sua natura." Goclenius, *Lexicon*, 312.

Chapter Five

I

Now, finally: In what sense might the principle of the truth of all things relate to anthropology or even contribute to a deeper understanding of human nature? And what exactly would this principle say about man?

Two specific aspects defining the truth of all things must be considered before all else. First: truth here means a transcendental property of all that is, a property that encompasses and surpasses *all* species and categories of existing things, so that it is impossible to construe anything as real and not also as true. Second: transcendental truth as a property of all that exists entails the orientation of every being toward another being (which distinguishes ontological truth from the other transcendentals: *ens, res* and *unum*). More specifically: the concept of transcendental truth affirms the relatedness of every being to the *inner core* of another being, the knowing mind (distinguishing, this time, ontological truth from *aliquid*, which also implies a relatedness, but only as extrinsic delimitation of one being from the other and not involving the inner core of another being).

To affirm that every existing thing in its being is ordered toward the inner core of another being, "this is possible only if there really exists some entity essentially designed to conform with everything there is. Of such nature, indeed, is the human soul, which in a certain sense is all in all. . . . The soul, however, possesses the power of knowledge and of will. Conformity of being and will, then, is called 'good'. . . . Conformity of being and knowledge is called 'true'."[1] These lines,

---

[1] "Hoc quidem non potest esse nisi accipiatur aliquid quod natum sit convenire cum omni ente. Hoc autem est anima, quae quodammodo est omnia, sicut dicitur in III de Anima. In anima autem est vis cognitiva et appetitiva. Convenientiam ergo entis ad appetitum exprimit hoc nomen bonum. . . . Convenientiam vero entis ad intellectum exprimit hoc nomen verum." *Ver.* I, I.

once again taken from the amazing first article of Thomas Aquinas' *Quaestiones disputatae de veritate*, characterize the principle of the truth of all things as a statement on the nature of man.

What, indeed, is affirmed here? Precisely this: reality, any reality without exception, can only be called true—meaning: knowable—if the human soul possesses in itself the ability to know the totality of all things. Furthermore, reality as such—and so everything that has being—can only claim truth—that is: object-ivity—if in turn the subject-ivity of the knowing mind is seen as facing the totality of all that is. The principle of the truth of all things, therefore, expresses but one side of an essentially two-sided situation whose other side is this: "The mind by its nature is oriented to conform to all that has being."[2] The former cannot be conceived without assuming the latter; the former implies the latter as its foundation.

Thomas Aquinas here does not envision some abstract and ideal "mind", nor indeed God's knowing mind, but plainly man as such. This is demonstrated by his using the term "soul" in this context, *anima:* man's spirit or soul, inasmuch as it intrinsically forms and determines man's body as well. The soul, then, is for Thomas that entity without which we cannot conceive of truth as a property of all existing things. This position allowed Thomas at times to view and formulate—in the *Summa theologica* and elsewhere—the doctrine of the truth of all things specifically in connection with the soul's all-embracing relationship to the universe of all existing things: "All things are knowable insofar as they have being. For this reason is it said that the soul in a certain sense is all in all."[3] And further: "Since all that is expressed [in the transcendentals] beyond *being* pertains to reality in view of the soul,

---

[2] *Ver.* I, I.

[3] "Unumquodque autem, inquantum habet de esse, intantum est cognoscibile. Et propter hoc dicitur, quod anima est quodammodo omnia." *ST* I, 16, 3. Regarding the "identity" between the subject and the object of knowledge, cf. Pieper, *Reality and the Good*, 115ff.

which in a certain sense is all in all, we consequently obtain the concepts of *truth* and of *goodness*. For the soul possesses a two-fold power: to know and to love; the one enables it to know all things, the other to love all things."[4]

It should be noted here that this combination of the two aspects—the truth of all things on the one hand, the orientation of the human mind toward the totality of things on the other—that this connection is stated in explicit terms only in the writings of Thomas Aquinas. His position on this subject appears to be entirely original. True, the statement about the soul being somehow all in all[5] and also the concept of the truth of all things[6] originated with Aristotle. In Plato's *Dialogues*, and in Plotinus'[7] or Augustine's writings as well, we may indeed be able to discover the more or less succinct and precise formulation of one or the other of these two notions. Relating one to the other, however, uncovering the profound depth where they both spring from the same root, this is the intellectual achievement of Thomas Aquinas alone. Nobody preceded him in this, and nobody after him, it seems, would follow his lead.

The two-sidedness we mentioned should not be understood simply in a univocal sense, though. It does not mean, of course, that reality relates to the knowing mind in exactly the same manner as the mind relates to reality. The interrelation of "world" and "mind" is not conceived as identical in both directions. As was mentioned already several times, the relationship of an object to the knowing mind exists in concrete fact only in the act of knowing itself, by which the object's latent knowability is transformed into actual knowledge. The

---

[4] "Si autem illud, quod additur super ens, sequatur ens in comparatione ad animan, quae quodammodo est omnia (in anima enim duplex est potentia, intellectus scilicet et voluntas, quarum altera omnia cognoscere potest, altera autem amare), sic accipiuntur verum et bonum." *De natura generis*, chap. 2.

[5] Aristotle, *De anima* 3, 8, 431b.

[6] Aristotle, *Metaphysics* 2, 1, 993b.

[7] In *Theologia Aristotelis* (cf. chap. 1, no. 5) we find: "The mind is indeed all things." Quoted from Guttmann, *Isaac ben Salomon*, 34.

objects in and of themselves do not actively establish a relationship with the mind; rather, they are passively "ordered"
toward it. It is the mind that in its most specific activity "relates" to reality; more precisely, it is the mind that changes an
already existing but only potential relationship between objective reality and subjective cognition into actual fact. (This latter aspect should definitely be emphasized: it confirms the
teaching that the mind does not "create" the subject–object relationship but is rather by nature, and so—as it were—also
"passively", ordered toward the world of objects.)

Reality and the knowing mind, then, are not to be conceived as the two separate though somehow interrelated
hemispheres of all that is. Instead, reality is the field of reference for the mind, and the mind is the active (more precisely:
the actively accepting and receiving) center of this field of reference. All that is, is true.

This now means: all existing things, inasmuch as they have
being and through their being, are positioned within the
knowing soul's field of reference; and this field of reference,
the "world" of man the knower, is nothing less extensive or
significant than the total universe of all that is. Being able to
know means to exist in relation to, and be immersed in, all
that is. The mind, and the mind alone, is *capax universi* [ca-
pable of grasping the universe].

It pertains to the nature of all things that by being known
they are being "grasped" and thus become the prey and property of the knowing mind. The nature of the mind, on the
other hand, lies in its ability to "grasp" in turn all things.

2

The statement about the mind being "designed to conform to
all that is" finds a surprising further explication through another element of Thomas Aquinas' world view.

The *Summa contra Gentiles* contains a magnificently sweep-
ing chapter that sheds a penetrating light on the entire archi-

tecture of the world, from rock to angel and even to the mystery of the Trinity.[8] In this chapter we read: "'Each thing, according to its specific nature, manifests itself in a specific manner. And the higher a thing ranks in the order of being, the more intrinsic is its manifestation.'"[9] The more an entity is able to dwell within itself, the higher its rank in the order of being. The highest form of selfness effects the highest rank of being and essence.

This reflection now offers a further explanation regarding the mind's power to "grasp the universe". For the notion of "having an intrinsic existence" corresponds to "being able to relate", so that the most comprehensive ability to relate — namely, the power to "conform to all that is" — implies at the same time also the highest form of intrinsic existence, of selfness. This connection still requires some further discussion and clarification.

The concept of "intrinsic existence" refers to that dynamic core of an entity from which all active manifestations originate and toward which all endurance and receptivity are focused and directed. An entity endowed with an intrinsic existence is ontologically a "subject", a self-contained unified being. If every existing thing is "one", then the notion of "intrinsic existence" means a more intense inner unity; and so, the being with an intrinsic existence constitutes a heightened and self-contained "oneness". Inorganic objects are without intrinsic existence; at most we can speak of a rock's "inside" in a material sense — even though any inorganic object still is a substance, an existing being, and as such prefigures an intrinsic

---

[8] The chapter in question is part of the exposition on the Trinity and is entitled, "Quomodo accipienda sit generatio in divinis et quae de Filio Dei dicuntur in scripturis." *CG* 4, 11. (A German translation of the more important section of this chapter is found in Pieper, *Auskunft*, 45ff.) The biologist Hans André, *Wesensunterschied*. bases his excellent brief study on the contents of this chapter.

[9] "Secundum diversitatem naturarum diversus emanationis modus invenitur in rebus; et quanto aliqua natura est altior, tanto id, quod ex ea emanat, magis est intimum." *CG* 4, 11.

existence proper. Plants do possess a true intrinsic existence; animals even more so. The most genuine and highest form of intrinsic existence is the spirit-endowed self.

But, indeed, the term "intrinsic" directly presupposes also what is "extrinsic" or "the world", what is around and outside. Only in reference to an inside can there be an outside. Without a self-contained "subject" there can be no "object". Relating-to, conforming-with, being-oriented-toward—all these notions presuppose an inside starting point. True, a rock, too, is "with" and "beside" other things "in" the world; but these "relational" prepositions "with, beside, in" do not denote an intrinsic relatedness of the rock to its surrounding objects. It is essential for any genuine relationship to originate from an inside and extend toward an outside. The pebble in a brook, in itself, does not "relate" to its surroundings nor to the world. The flower, in contrast, endowed with true intrinsic existence, truly "relates" to its surroundings: the nutrient minerals surrounding its roots, for example, are "close" not only in a physical sense; they form an integral part of a plant's circle of life.

Expressions like relating-to and reaching-out-toward indeed bring out the genuine, active meaning of the term "relatedness". The higher the form of intrinsic existence, the more developed becomes the relatedness with reality, also the more profound and comprehensive becomes the sphere of this relatedness: namely, the world. And the deeper such relations penetrate the world of reality, the more intrinsic becomes the respective subject's existence.

The world of a plant does not extend beyond what it touches. The world of an animal reaches as far and deep as sensory perception can reach. The world of the spirit-endowed self, a person's "I", spans the totality of all that is; the world of the spirit is the universe of being.[10]

---

[10] Cf. Pieper, *Philosophieren*, 36–44.

Thomas Aquinas, considering the ascending order of these different "worlds", assigned each of them explicitly to a corresponding potency or power of the human soul itself: "The higher a potency [of the soul], the more comprehensive is the sphere of objects toward which it is ordered. The entire range over which the soul's activity extends can be ordered into three levels. One of the soul's powers concerns only the body to which a soul is joined; this kind of power is called the vegetative faculty, and its activity affects only the body to which this soul is joined. Then there is in the soul another kind of power that relates to a wider sphere; namely, to all material objects accessible through the senses and not just relating to the body to which the soul is joined. And a third kind of power in the soul is directed toward an even more comprehensive sphere of objects: not only toward all material things, but toward all that exists."[11]

To sum it up, then: to have (or to be) an "intrinsic existence" means "to be able to relate" and "to be the sustaining subject at the center of a field of reference". The hierarchy of existing things, being equally a hierarchy of intrinsic existences, corresponds on each level to the intensity and extension of the respective relationship in their power, character and domain. Consequently, the spirit-based self, the highest form of being and of intrinsic existence as well, must have the most intensive power to relate and the most comprehensive domain of relatedness: the universe of all existing things. These two aspects, combined—dwelling most intensively within itself, and being *capax universi*, able to grasp the universe—together constitute the essence of the spirit. Any definition of "spirit" will have to contain these two aspects as its core.[12]

---

[11] "Quanto enim potentia est altior, tanto respicit universalius objectum. . . . Est autem aliud genus potentiarum animae, quod respicit non solum corpus sensibile, sed etiam universaliter omne ens." *ST* I, 78, 1. Cf. also: "Quanto potentia est superior, tanto ad plura se extendit." *ST* I, 77, 3 ad 4.

[12] "The human mind, in the very core of its nature, is receptivity, readiness, openness for all reality. . . . The human mind is ultimately the pure receptor of all that is." Rohner, "Grundproblem", 1083.

3

In various ways, and in almost all of his major works, Thomas
Aquinas states that the human mind is ordered toward the totality of all that exists. The *Summa contra Gentiles* says: "Spirit-
endowed beings possess a higher affinity to the whole of reality than other beings. Every spiritual substance namely, in a
certain sense, is all in all, insofar as it is able, through its cognitive power, to comprehend all there is. Any other substance,
in contrast, enjoys but an incomplete participation in the
realm of being."[13] The *Summa theologica* states: "Man's yearn-
ing is to know what is ultimate and perfect",[14] and the *Quaestiones disputatae de veritate:*

> It has been said that the soul is in a certain sense all in all; for
> its nature is directed toward universal knowledge. In this man-
> ner is it possible for the perfection of the entire world to be
> present in one single being. Consequently, the highest perfec-
> tion attainable for the soul would be reached when the soul
> comprehends the entire order of the universe and its principles,
> according to the philosophers. They therefore see precisely in
> this the ultimate end of man, which—as we believe—will be
> realized in the beatific vision; for, as Gregory says, "what
> would those not see who see him who sees all?"[15]

[13] "Naturae autem intellectuales majorem habent affinitatem ad totum
quam aliae naturae; nam unaquaeque intellectualis substantia est quodammodo omnia, in quantum totius entis comprehensiva est suo intellectu; quaelibet autem alia substantia particularem solam entis participationem habet."
CG 3, 112.
[14] "Homo desiderat cognoscere aliquod totum et perfectum." *ST* I, 2,
32, 2.
[15] "Dicitur animam esse quodammodo omnia, quia nata est omnia cognoscere. Et secundum hunc modum possibile est, ut in una re totius universi perfectio existat. Unde haec est ultima perfectio, ad quam anima potest perve-
nire, secundum philosophos, ut in ea describatur totus ordo universi et
causarum ejus; in quo etiam finem ultimum hominis posuerunt, qui, secundum nos, erit in visione Dei, quia secundum Gregorium 'Quid est, quod non
videant, qui videntem omnia vident?' " *Ver.* 2, 2. It is, therefore, not entirely
correct to say, as Hans Meyer does, referring to *Ver.* 2, 2.: "Thomas agrees

And again the *Summa theologica:* "The soul of man, in a certain
sense, becomes all in all, depending on experience and insight.
In this respect, beings endowed with cognitive ability somehow resemble God himself in whom all things preexist, as
Dionysius says."[16]

4

At this point we do well to consider—in passing, as it
were—Arnold Gehlen's anthropological study, so much discussed [in its time].[17] His point of departure, though this point
only, lies entirely within the great tradition of Western philosophy. Gehlen's basic thesis, rightly directed against von
Uexküll,[18] states that "man alone possesses, not just a sur-

---

with Aristotle as he sees the highest perfection of the soul consisting in having
the entire order of the universe and its principles engraved in it." Meyer, *Thomas von Aquin*, 214. On the contrary, Thomas here does not so much join the
"philosophers" as rather Gregory, the Church Father! He disassociates himself from them even more in a similar passage: *Ver.* 20, 3.

[16] "Anima hominis fit omnia quodammodo secundum sensum et intellectum, in quo cognitionem habentia ad Dei similitudinem quodammodo ap-
propinquant, in quo omnia praeexistunt, sicut Dionysius dicit (*De div. nom.*
5.1)." *ST* I, 80, 1. Once again, a passage from Geothe should be quoted:
"This (soul-like organ, the Monad) desires not only to mirror the surrounding totality but, as much as possible, to become itself this surrounding totality. For that reason does every higher organism, by its nature, take possession
of the lower ones, transporting them into its own essence: plants absorb inorganic matter simply through growing and changing; animals absorb plants
through growing, changing and consuming; and man not only absorbs animals and plants into his inner essence through growing, changing and consuming, but at the same time he collects into the domain of his existence everything that is of a lower order; for his nature, like a highly polished mirror,
is the most sensitive of all." *Italienische Reise* (Rome, 1788), chap. 3, "Über
die bildende Nachahmung des Schönen", a text authored by K.P. Moritz.
Hildebrandt is justified in his observation that Goethe acknowledged this exposition by Moritz "as his own thinking, sharing the credit for it". Hildebrandt, *Goethe*, 245.

[17] Gehlen, *Mensch*.

[18] Because I am in no position to judge von Uexküll's biological accom-
plishments, I have no intention of questioning them. But he naively steps beyond biology when, for example, he puts the habitat of animals on the same

rounding, but 'world' as such".[19] The animal is adapted to a specific environment and so also limited by it; man's environment, in contrast, is the totality of all that exists, so that man, by nature, is *weltoffen*, oriented toward "the world".[20] Max Scheler, indeed *before* Gehlen, has expressed the very same thought in almost identical words: "Such a 'spiritual' being is . . . not tied to a particular environment but rather—shall we say—*weltoffen*, oriented toward 'the world'. Such a being possesses 'world' as such."[21]

Gehlen, however, immediately robs himself of the potential benefits implied in his correct starting point. Caught in an anti-metaphysical, "anthropobiological" dogmatism, he misinterprets man's openness to the world as an expression, even a consequence,[22] of man's organic imperfection and "lack of specific natural means" and so as a "basically negative reality".[23] Gehlen emphasizes that the distinction between specific adaptation and universal openness "provides between man and animal a clear differentiation that is *not* based on properties like consciousness or spirit".[24] This misconception on Gehlen's part is all the more remarkable for employing the very same distinction used to differentiate between beings that are, or are not, endowed with spirit. How far removed from all Western philosophical tradition is such thinking! It ac-

---

level as the world of man, without qualification or distinction. Generally, whenever von Uexküll's opinions touch on philosophy, they are marked by inadmissible simplifications. Rothacker, "Kultur-anthropologie", 157ff., an essay pursuing von Uexküll's ideas, also disregards the metaphysical distinction between man and animal.

[19] Gehlen, *Mensch*, 20. Gehlen subsequently has further elaborated this thesis. Cf. Gehlen, "Systematik", 18ff.

[20] Gehlen, *Mensch*, 24.

[21] Scheler, *Stellung des Menschen*, 47.

[22] "But here we see the 'pattern' of a being that is organically deficient, *therefore* (!) universally open, *that is* (!), not naturally at home in any specific and strictly defined habitat." Gehlen, *Mensch*, 24.

[23] "In saying that 'man exists unto the world' . . . we really do express a negative reality." Gehlen, *Mensch*, 24.

[24] Gehlen, *Mensch*, 24.

knowledges man's distinctive spirit-based ability to grasp the world and then forgets or denies the aspect of the spirit![25]

It may be interesting, even surprising, to learn how the simultaneous presence of organic "shortcomings" and spirit-based universal openness is explicitly treated as an anthropological question in Thomas Aquinas' *Summa theologica*. There we find the following "objection":

> The spiritual soul is the most perfect soul of all. But realizing how the bodies of all the other animate beings are endowed with some natural protection, like fur for clothes and hoofs for shoes, and are also endowed with natural weapons, like claws, teeth and horns, then it would seem that the spiritual soul should not have been united to such a deficient body that lacks all those endowments.

Thomas replies to his own objection:

> The spiritual soul, being able to know the essences of things, possesses a potency unto the infinite. It would therefore be entirely inappropriate for nature to shackle the soul either with specific instinctive attitudes or with specific endowments for defense or protection the way other animate beings are constrained, and whose souls are limited in potency and apprehension to a well-defined particular area. In place of all this, man is naturally endowed with reason and furnished with hands, which together are the ultimate tools of all tools, allowing man to fashion instruments of any kind and for an infinity of purposes.[26]

---

[25] Gehlen's study is extensively discussed in the notes of the previous edition of this book.

[26] "Anima intellectiva est perfectissima animarum. Cum igitur aliorum animalium corpora habeant naturaliter insita tegumenta, puta pilorum loco vestium et ungularum loco calceamentorum; habeant etiam arma naturaliter sibi data, sicut ungues, dentes et cornua: videtur quod anima intellectiva non debuerit uniri corpori imperfecto, tamquam talibus auxiliis privato. Anima intellectiva, quia est universalium comprehensiva, habet virtutem ad infinita: et ideo non potuerunt sibi determinari a natura vel determinatae existimationes naturales, vel etiam determinata auxilia vel defensiorum vel tegumentorum sicut aliis animalibus, quorum animae habent apprehensionem et virtutem ad aliqua particularia determinata; sed loco horum omnium homo habet natu-

5

It is, of course, not only nor primarily the vaster physical extension that distinguishes the unlimited world of man from the specific habitat of the animal. Not only a more comprehensive but above all a qualitatively higher field of reference, as already mentioned, is the proper domain of man, the mind-endowed self. The capacity to reach a wider area is paired with a higher form of relating to reality.

The controversy concerning "open world versus specific environment" often ignores this dimension. The zoologist Paul Buchner, for example, in a small volume filled with intriguing biological findings, addresses Gehlen in this way:

> I fail to see an essential difference between the specific habitat of the animal and the universal world of man, a distinction Gehlen tries to establish. In this I agree entirely with von Uexküll, who was the first to study how living organisms interact with their environment. And if we consider the vast expanses of cosmic space that defy our investigations, then our own "world" will shrink considerably and become comparable to the "world" of that snail we mentioned.[27]

To deny essential differences here means to consider only the quantitative aspect and to forget that "all things spiritual are called 'great' according to the perfection of their nature; so also says Augustine, referring to a realm where things are not 'great' simply by their dimensions: there, 'being greater' means 'being more perfect'."[28]

---

raliter rationem et manus, quae sunt organa organorum, quia per ea homo potest sibi praeparare instrumenta infinitorum modorum et ad infinitos effectus." *ST* I, 76, 5 obj. 4 ad 4.

[27] Buchner, *Spezialisierung*, 38.

[28] "Sic relinquitur res spirituales magnas dici secundum modum suae completionis. Nam et Agustinus (*Trin.* 6, 9) dicit, quod in his, quae non mole magna sunt, hoc est majus esse, quod est melius esse." *CG* I, 43.

It is not merely the "totality of all things" but equally the "nature of things"[29] that constitutes the realm of the mind. We are able to reach—which does not mean comprehend—the essence of things, and because of this we find ourselves empowered to attain the totality of things as well.

Just as the totality of the created world, for classical metaphysics, is "universal" in character, so also is the nature of all things, a nature that is accessible only through the cognitive power of the mind. The essence of every existing thing is itself "universal".

This fundamental pronouncement of traditional Western metaphysics requires some brief reflection here. Precisely at this point there come into sight certain important elements of the conceptual system through which the tradition tried to explain the entire edifice of the world. We have to limit ourselves, of course, to a short description and interpretation; it would require a more voluminous study to bring to light the intricate web of this principle's far-reaching roots.

What, precisely, is stated here? First this: *Omnis forma, in quantum huiusmodi, universalis est:*[30] the essence of a thing is universal in character, transcending all specific, individual properties. Second: the mind alone possesses the cognitive power to reach these universal essences, which to the senses must remain concealed and inaccessible. Indeed, the mind's cognitive power is so much oriented toward the universal essences of things that these alone—in a strict sense—constitute its proper object: "The only objects our mind apprehends directly are universal essences",[31] while it "cannot perceive in any primary and immediate manner the specifics of a given material object";[32] "strictly speaking, our mind does not per-

---

[29] "Intellectus solus apprehendit essentias rerum." *ST* I, 57, 1 ad 2.

[30] *Ver.* 2, 6.

[31] "Intellectus noster directe non est cognoscitivus nisi universalium." *ST* I, 86, 1.

[32] "Singulare in rebus materialibus intellectus noster directe et primo cognoscere non potest." *ST* I, 86, 1.

ceive individual properties but only universal essences".[33] It is, therefore, their abstract and universal character that makes the essential natures of material things knowable and intelligible to the mind.

And, third, there is the much-discussed statement by Thomas Aquinas that sees the singular and specific properties of an object flow, not from its essential form, but from its *materia;* that is, from the form's counterpart, the matter that is molded and in-formed by an object's essence.[34] This *principium individuationis* [principle of individuation], too, is rooted in the concept of essences as being universal in character.

No matter how difficult it may be for us moderns to appreciate these teachings, their importance for the total picture of our study becomes immediately evident: the fact, namely, that it is not just a mere linguistic coincidence when traditional metaphysics uses the same predicate, "universal", for both the *essence* of things and the *totality* of things.

The universal world of man is not constituted simply in the vaster expansion of the same reality accessible also to the animal. Rather, it is by knowing the *essence* of things that man gains access to the totality of the universe as well, for this essence is universal in character. An animal's perception is incapable of reaching the universal essence of things, and precisely *for this reason* is the animal bound and limited to a small and specific sector of reality only. The ability to recognize the intrinsic nature of things provides a perspective from which the all-including totality of the world as a whole becomes accessible and discernible. "*Because* the spiritual soul can grasp universal essences, it possesses a potential unto infinity."[35]

All this now is intimately connected with the concept of the truth of all things and its anthropological implications. The

[33] "Relinquitur quod intellectus noster, per se loquendo, singularia non cognoscat, sed universalia tantum." *Ver.* 2, 6.

[34] *Ver.* 2, 6 ad 1.

[35] "Anima intellectiva, quia est universalium comprehensiva, habet virtutem ad infinita." *ST* I, 76, 5 ad 4.

"second" aspect of this concept has been determined as the knowability of all things—knowability for man, that is. Because, however, the knowability of all things, their intelligibility, is based on their universal essences, it follows that the very concept of the truth of all things already implies, virtually but nonetheless in a real sense, the reference to the fundamentals of reality, man's one and rightful world.

At this point we have completed the circle of questions and answers and have reached the goal we originally sought. All things are true; they are known and knowable—known to God's mind, knowable to the human mind: this is a statement not only about the essential structure of all things but about their "intrinsic openness". This statement of the truth of all things equally affirms the power of God's knowledge, which causes all things to be and to be translucent, making them real and therefore knowable. This statement also affirms that the human mind, by its very nature, is ordered toward the totality of all that exists, and this by the Creator's dispensation, who has disposed the universe toward the mind and the mind toward the universe, making reality knowable and the mind eager to know.

What, then, is said here? Man, because of his mind and inasmuch as he is endowed with spirit, dwells in the midst of the totality of all that is. The human mind, by its nature and created structure, finds itself in this preordained orientation toward the universe in the same way and at the same moment it finds its own existence. And the mind's inborn ability to "reach the whole" is actuated already in each single instance of cognition; for the light that makes any individual object intelligible is the same light that permeates the universe. All this, then, is the anthropological meaning, the affirmation about the nature of man, contained in the principle: *omne ens est verum*—all that is, is true.

CONCLUSION

Let us add, as some kind of conclusion, three brief considerations. They are designed to stake out, one final time, the perimeters of our findings; secure them against misinterpretations; point to some implications; and underline the anthropological significance involved by showing how the ontological doctrine of man's universal openness leads into the field of human ethics.

I

Never will man be able to comprehend fully—that is, know totally and perfectly—the inner nature of things. And never will man's mind be able to measure out completely the totality of the universe.[1] These two statements apparently contradict what has been said so far, yet only apparently: they form a necessary completion. To do justice to the masters of traditional metaphysics, who definitely were no proponents of rationalistic Enlightenment, we must not stop at the affirmation, "the knowing mind reaches the very essence of things",[2] but immediately be aware of this qualification: "Our cognitive power is so imperfect that not even the nature of one single gnat was ever entirely understood by any philosopher."[3]

Knowledge of the *essence* and the *totality* of things is man's prerogative within the "promise of hope". This means: any cognitive effort will indeed always be a positive advance, but only like a step on a longer journey, and will in principle not be destined for frustration; still, it will always and ever anew remain preliminary, incomplete, proclaiming "not yet". "In

---

[1] "Non enim [homo] in sua cognitione naturali habet omnium naturalium notitiam." *ST* I, 91, 1.

[2] "Intellectus vero penetrat usque ad rei essentiam." *ST* II, 1, 31, 5.

[3] "Cognito nostra est adeo debilis, quod nullus philosophus potuit unquam perfecte investigare naturam unius muscae." *Symb.*

any cognitive act, our mind stretches into infinity"[4]—equally meaning the breadth of the universe and the depth of any essence: the "limit" of knowledge is never attained, neither in objective fullness nor in subjective satisfaction. Man, therefore, is by nature someone who always, and ever anew, can reach for higher perfection, someone endowed with limitless potentials, even for happiness. Yet those potentials, the moment they become real, already point to new horizons that lie beyond. It is precisely this condition that shows man as being *capax universi*, able to grasp the universe—so much so that even the universe, which in the end is not "all there is", fails to fill man's soul.

2

Man is not only his mind. Whenever Thomas Aquinas compares man with animals, he calls the latter "the other sense-endowed beings".[5] Thomas evidently sees man "not merely as a soul, but as an intrinsic unity of body and soul".[6] He goes so far as to assert, utterly against our common conception of "medieval thinking", that "the soul united with the body is more in the image of God than when separate; for [in this union] it realizes its own essence more perfectly."[7] For Thomas, the interrelation between body and soul is captured in a formula that stems from the Aristotelian tradition,[8] was almost canonized in the High Middle Ages[9] and has little by

---

[4] "Intellectus noster intelligendo aliquid in infinitum extenditur." *CG* 1, 43.

[5] For example: *ST* I, 76, 5 ad 4.

[6] "Manifestum est quod homo non est anima tantum, sed aliquid compositum ex anima et corpore." *ST* I, 75, 4.

[7] *Pot.* 5, 10 ad 5.

[8] Aristotle, *De anima* 2, 1.

[9] The Council of Vienne (1311–12) adopted, e.g., this definition: "definientes, ut cunctis nota sit fidei sincerae veritas ac praecludatur universis erroribus aditus, ne subintrent, quod quisquis deinceps asserere, defendere seu tenere pertinaciter praesumpserit, quod anima rationalis seu intellectiva non sit forma corporis humani per se et essentialiter, tanquam haereticus sit

little been rediscovered in our own age: *anima forma corporis*— the soul is the form-giving principle of the body. On the one hand, this formula clearly asserts the priority of the form-giving spiritual soul; on the other, it also affirms that man's spirit is ordered toward the body and the senses and thus toward the material world: "The senses are the primary sources of our knowledge, and for this reason do all our discernments somehow and necessarily refer back to the senses."[10] Thomas goes even further: "Although divine revelation raises us to a level where we perceive realities otherwise hidden from us, we are nonetheless never lifted so high as to perceive these realities in any other way than through the world of the senses."[11] Still, it is the spiritual soul that "shapes" also the functions of the senses; for "strictly speaking, it is not the senses that perceive, but man perceives through them."[12]

What, then, does all this mean for our main topic? It means two things. First, man's world is not merely and neatly the rather abstract "totality" of all there is, but an intermingling of specific "surroundings" and universal "world". Max Scheler conceives man's "universal openness" as total freedom from the specifics of a habitat, as if man were "a being surpassing himself and the world",[13] really not bound any more to profess, "I am part of the world, I am embedded in the world."[14] In this, Scheler shows himself a disciple of philosophical Idealism, nearly making man into a pure spirit. Such a romanticizing approach, redefining man in terms of spirit alone,[15] is utterly alien to the realistic outlook of tradi-

---

censendus." *Constitutio de Summa Trinitate et fide catholica.* Cf. Denzinger, *Enchiridion*, no. 481.

[10] *Ver.* 12, 3 ad 2.

[11] *Trin.* 6, 3.

[12] "Non enim, propter loquendo, sensus aut intellectus cognoscunt, sed homo per utrumque." *Ver.* 2, 6 ad 3.

[13] Scheler, *Stellung des Menschen*, 58.

[14] Scheler, *Stellung des Menschen*, 106.

[15] At the conclusion of Scheler's reasoning, however, this "spiritualization" changes to the spirit's alleged dependency on the "vital impetus". On

tional anthropology. This realistic outlook knows and accepts that man, in order to function as man, needs to move within the structure of accustomed surroundings; that he needs the familiar environment of his daily work and activities; in short, that he needs the specific, physical world close to his senses. Because man is indeed not "pure" spirit, he cannot live exclusively *vis-à-vis de l'univers*, always facing "the whole world"; he cannot simply live "beneath the star", he also needs a roof over his head.

Secondly, however, it insults the dignity of man's spirit to lead a life so much confined and imprisoned within narrow considerations of immediate usefulness that his own small environment utterly ceases to be a window on the larger "world". To be thus totally absorbed in a mere fragment of reality, to "function" rather than live, is not human; yet to be so tempted is indeed all too human. However necessary the roof over the head may be: for life to be truly human it seems indispensable that every so often the domain of practical work and effectiveness be shaken up and brought down to size by the challenge, disturbing yet fruitful, coming from the world's ultimate reality—the totality of universal essences, mirrors of the eternal Ideas in God.

3

This leads us to a third and final consideration: an attitude of willing readiness for an unlimited variety of challenges and tasks seems to correspond best to man's intrinsic orientation toward the universe of all that is. This ethical attitude of openness, which readily acknowledges what is required in a given situation, was seen by Thomas Aquinas as one of the foundations for a truly human life, especially in his teachings on the virtue of prudence. For him prudence ranks as the first, the

---

the whole, this particular work—the last one to be published by Scheler himself—appears strikingly inadequate in thought and expression.

"mother", of the other cardinal virtues[16] of justice, fortitude and temperance. This concept of prudence, of course, does not make it ideal human behavior to remain uncommitted, ever neutral and ready to do anything, as it were. The realm of prudence is the realm of all that lies at man's disposal, and indeed it does not include the ultimate ends of man's life. "Not the final goals are we to determine, but only the ways leading there."[17] Thus it is not the task of prudence to decide on life's final goals and determine the basic aspirations of human nature. Rather, the virtue of prudence consists in finding, here and now, the right approach to attain those goals and aspirations. Prudence does not answer the question whether I ought to be just or not; instead, it answers the question of how I can pursue justice here and now. Accepting the goal, having the right objective, acting with "good intention"—these are the preconditions, the preceding attitudes, of any prudent decision. Without that lasting determination to pursue what is right, going beyond the immediate situation, all efforts to find out what would be prudent and good here and now amount to nothing more than self-deception and empty busywork. Important here is that all inner determination, transcending specific circumstances, be indeed aimed at the true and highest goals of man's life. These goals themselves should not require, again and again, our personal decision. It could happen, however, that someone "exempts" from conscientious consideration even those points that by their very nature belong in the domain of prudence; that is, the domain of all those contingent things to be pondered and decided in each case and in view of each specific situation. This is a quite common accommodation on a factual and practical level, to fashion for oneself some sort of moral enclave to escape some of life's particular demands. Not only that, but such an approach is found even

[16] *Sent.* 3, d. 33, 2, 5.
[17] "De fine non est consilium, sed solum de his quae sunt ad finem." *ST* II, 1, 14, 2. Thomas is drawing here from Aristotle, as he does quite often in his reflections on ethics.

on a theoretical level, justified and legitimated in certain systems and theories of ethics and education, say, through authoritarian prescription of "ideals" and "models" or else through casuistical directives. But in no other manner are the noble purposes of life achieved and man's ethical call fulfilled than by struggling, in each specific case, for the appropriate answer to a reality whose ultimate extent we cannot measure once and for all and whose inner nature is marked by unlimited, changing diversity. Plato, in his ninth letter, says: "One part of our life belongs to our country, another to our parents, another to others we love. The largest portion, however, is dedicated to all those moments, coming to us quite accidentally, when we are challenged to accomplish something good."

The spirit-based self, ordered as it is toward the whole of reality, is in its very essence called to face with an attitude of receptive, unbiased openness this universality of its world, revealed in countless concrete experiences. Only in this way, indeed, can man realize his own destiny, a destiny not of his own invention, a destiny, moreover, whose final features he may not even behold beforehand. Nobody is able to anticipate his personal destiny and set it up as his "ideal": man is positioned too much in the midst of a world that constantly deals out surprises beyond all presumed knowledge; man is living too much face to face with the absolute of it all, so that his own inner boundlessness constitutes but the counterpart to an unfathomable world.

Yet this world itself, according to its inner nature, is beholden to the creative word spoken in God's knowing mind, and there, by God's "artistry", its primordial ideas have and are life. For the world of all existing things "is placed between two knowing minds",[18] the mind of God and the mind of man. And precisely from there, as classical Western metaphysics has always known, springs *the truth of all things.*

[18] "Res naturalis, inter duos intellectus constituta, secundum adaequationem ad utrumque vera dicitur." *Ver.* 1, 2.

BIBLIOGRAPHY

Alexander von Hales. *Summa theologica.* Quaracchi, 1924ff.

André, Hans. *Der Wesensunterschied von Pflanze, Tier und Mensch.* Habelschwerdt, 1922.

Anselm of Canterbury. *Dialogus de veritate.* Vol. 158 of *Migne Patrologia Latina.*

Averroës. *Die Metaphysik des Averroës.* Translated from the Arabic and explained by Max Horten. Halle, 1912.

Avicenna. *Metaphysics Compendium ex Arabo Latinum reddidit Nematallah Carame.* Rome, 1926.

——. *Die Metaphysik Avicennas.* Translated and explained by Max Horten. Halle, New York, 1907.

——. "Die Psychologie des Ibn Sina." Translated and edited by S. Landauer. *Zeitschr. der Deutschen Morgenländischen Gesellschaft,* vol. 29 (1876).

Bacon, Francis. *The Works of Francis Bacon.* Collected and edited by J. Spedding, R. L. Ellis, D. D. Heath. *Philosophical Works,* vols. 1–5. London, 1889ff.

Baeumker, Clemens. *Witelo.* Münster, 1908.

Baumgarten, Alexander Gottlieb. *Metaphysica.* 5th ed. Halle, 1768.

Bochenski, J. M. *Formale Logik.* Freiburg-München, 1956.

Buchner, Paul. *Spezialisierung und Entwicklung.* Leipzig, 1940.

Clasen, Carl T. *Versuch einer systematischen Erschliessung der Quaestiones disputatae de veritate des hl. Thomas von Aquin.* Dissertation. Mayen, 1935.

Denzinger, H. *Enchiridion symbolorum, definitionum et declarationum de rebus fidei et morum.* Edited by J. B. Umberg, 18th–20th ed. Freiburg im Breisgau, 1932.

Descartes, R. *Meditationes de prima philosophia.* Vol. 7 of the *Oeuvres de Descartes.* Paris, 1904.

——. *Principia philosophiae.* Vol. 8 of the *Oeuvres de Descartes.* Paris, 1905.

Dessauer, Philipp. *Wahrheit als Weg.* München, 1946.

Domet de Vorges. *Abrégé de Métaphysique: Etude historique et critique des doctrines de métaphysique scolastique.* 2 vols. Paris, 1906.

Dreyer, Hans. *Der Begriff Geist in der deutschen Philosophie von Kant bis Hegel.* Berlin, 1908.

Dunin-Borkowski, Stanislaus von. *Spinoza.* Vol. 3. Münster, 1935.

——. *Spinoza nach dreihundert Jahren.* Berlin-Bonn, 1932.

Duns Scotus. *Collationes seu Disputationes subtilissimae.* Vol. 3, treatise 6 of *Opera omnia.* Lugduni, 1639.

——. *In XII libros Metaphysicorum Aristotelis expositio.* Vol. 4 of *Opera omnia.* Lugduni, 1639.

——. *Commentaria Oxoniensia ad IV libros Magistri Sententiarum.* Quaracchi, 1912f.

Endres, J. A. *Forschungen zur Geschichte der frühmittelalterlichen Philosophie.* Münster, 1915.

——. "Die Stellung des Menschen im Kosmos." *Divus Thomas* 19 (1941).

Erdmann, Benno. "Mitteilungen über Kant's metaphysischen Standpunkt in der Zeit um 1774." *Philosophische Monatshefte* 20 (1884).

Ermecke, Gustav. *Die natürlichen Seinsgrundlagen der christlichen Ethik.* Paderborn, 1941.

Eschweiler, Karl. "Die Philosophie der spanischen Spätscholastik auf den deutschen Universitäten des siebzehnten Jahrhunderts." *Spanische Forschungen der Görresgesellschaft,* vol. 1. Münster, 1928.

——. *Die zwei Wege der neueren Theologie.* Augsburg, 1926.

Fischer, Joseph. *Die Erkenntnislehre Anselms von Canterbury.* Münster, 1911.

Freudenthal, Jakob. *Die Lebensgeschichte Spinozas in Quellenschriften, Urkunden und nichtamtlichen Nachrichten.* Leipzig, 1899.

Garcia, M. F. *Lexicon scholasticum.* Quaracchi, 1910.

Gehlen, Arnold. *Der Mensch: Seine Natur und seine Stellung in der Welt.* Berlin, 1940.

————. "Zur Systematik der Anthropologie." In *Systematische Philosophie*, by Nicolai Hartmann.

Getzeny, Heinrich. *Vom Wesen zum Sein: Der Weg der deutschen Philosophie der Gegenwart*. Hochland, 1936–37.

Goclenius, Rudolf. *Lexicon philosophicum, quo tanquam clave philosophiae fores aperiunter*. Frankfurt, 1613.

Goethe, J. W. *Autobiographische Schriften*. India paper ed. 3 vols. Leipzig: Inselverlag, no year.

————. *Farbenlehre*. Edited by Gunther Ipsen. India paper ed. Leipzig: Inselverlag, no year.

————. *Maximen und Reflexionen*. Edited by Günther Müller. Stuttgart, 1943.

Grabmann, M. *Die Werke des hl. Thomas von Aquin*. Münster, 1949.

Guardini, Romano. *Welt und Person: Versuche zur christlichen Lehre vom Menschen*. Würzburg, 1940.

Guttmann, Jakob. *Die philosophischen Lehren des Isaak ben Salomon Israeli*. Münster, 1911.

————. *Die Scholastik des 13. Jahrhunderts in ihren Beziehungen zum Judentum und zur jüdischen Literatur*. Breslau, 1902.

————. *Das Verhältnis des Thomas von Aquino zum Judentum und zur jüdischen Literatur*. Göttingen, 1891.

Haneberg, B. *Zur Erkenntnislehre von Ibn Sina und Albertus Magnus*. Abhandlungen der Bayr. Akademie der Wissenschaften, vol. 11. München, 1866.

Hartmann, Nicolai. *Das Problem des geistigen Seins*. Berlin-Leipzig, 1940.

Hartmann, Nicolai, ed. *Systematische Philosophie*. Stuttgart-Berlin, 1942.

Herder, J. G. von. *Briefe von und an Herder*. 3 vols. Edited by H. Düntzer. Leipzig, 1861–62.

Hettner, Hermann. *Geschichte der deutschen Literatur im achtzehnten Jahrhundert*. 4 vols. Leipzig, 1928.

Hildebrandt, Kurt. *Goethe: Seine Weltweisheit im Gesamtwerk*. Leipzig, 1941.

Hobbes, Thomas. *Opera philosophica*. Edited by G. Molesworth. Vols. 1–5. London, 1839.

Hufnagel, Alfons. *Studien zur Entwicklung des thomistischen Erkenntnisbegriffes im Anschluss an das Correctorium 'Quare'.* Münster, 1935.

Jansen, Bernhard. *Die Geschichte der Erkenntnislehre in der neueren Philosophie bis Kant.* Paderborn, 1940.

———. *Die scholastische Philosophie des 17. Jahrhunderts.* Phil. Jahrb. d. Görresgesellschaft, vol. 50 (1937).

Kant, Immanuel. *Kritik der reinen Vernunft.* Edited by R. Schmidt. Leipzig, 1944.

Klasmeier, Wilhelm. *Die Transzendentalienlehre des Franz Suarez.* Dissertation. Würzburg, 1939.

Knittermeyer, Hinrich. *Der Terminus transzendental in seiner historischen Entwicklung bis zu Kant.* Dissertation. Marburg, 1920.

Kremer, R. "La synthèse thomiste de la vérité". *Revue Néoscolastique de Philosophie* 35 (1933).

Kühle, Heinrich. "Die Lehre Alberts des Grossen von den Transzendentalien." In *Philosophia perennis*, edited by J. von Rintelen, 2 vols. Regensburg, 1930.

Lasswitz, Kurd. *Geschichte der Atomistik vom Mittelalter bis Newton.* 2 vols. Hamburg-Leipzig, 1889–90.

Leibniz, G. W. *Opera philosophica quae exstant latina gallica germanica omnia.* 2 parts. Berlin, 1839–40.

Leisegang, Hans. *Über die Behandlung des scholastischen Satzes 'Quodlibet ens est unum, verum, bonum seu perfectum' und seine Bedeutung in Kants Kritik der reinen Vernunft.* Kantstudien 20 (1915).

Lersch, Philipp. *Seele und Welt.* Leipzig, 1941.

Lotz, Johannes B. *Sein und Wert: Eine metaphysische Auslegung des Axioms: 'Ens et bonum convertuntur' im Raume der scholastischen Transzendentalienlehre.* Part 1, *Das Seiende und das Sein.* Paderborn, 1938.

Meyer, Hans. *Thomas von Aquin: Sein System und seine geistesgeschichtliche Stellung.* Bonn, 1938.

Nink, Caspar. *Sein und Erkennen*. Leipzig, 1938.

Oeing-Hanhoff, L. *Ens et unum convertuntur: Stellung und Ge-halt des Grundsatzes in der Philosophie des hl. Thomas von Aquin*. Münster, 1953.

Petermann, Bruno. *Wesensfragen seelischen Seins*. Leipzig, 1938.

Pieper, Josef. *Kurze Auskunft über Thomas von Aquin*. 3d ed. München, 1963.

――――. *Traktat über die Klugheit*. 7th ed. München, 1965.

――――. *Unaustrinkbares Licht: Das negative Element in der Welt-ansicht des Thomas von Aquin*. 2d ed. München, 1963.

――――. *Was heisst Philosophieren?* 5th ed. München, 1963.

――――. *Die Wirklichkeit und das Gute*. 7th ed. München, 1963. The second part of this present volume is an English translation of this work.

――――. *Zucht und Mass*. 9th ed. München, 1964.

Plessner, Helmuth. *Die Stufen des Organischen und der Mensch*. Berlin-Leipzig, 1928.

Prantl, C. *Geschichte der Logik im Abendlande*. 4 vols. Leipzig, 1855–1870. Reprinted, 3 vols. Graz, 1955.

Przywara, Erich. *Analogia entis: Metaphysik I*. München, 1932.

――――. *Ringen der Gegenwart: Gesammelte Aufsätze 1922 bis 1927*. 2 vols. Augsburg, 1929.

Rickert, Heinrich. "Die Erkenntnis der intelligiblen Welt und das Problem der Metaphysik." In *Unmittelbarkeit und Sinndeutung: Aufsätze zur Ausgestaltung des Systems der Philosophie*, by H. Rickert. Tübingen, 1939.

Rohner, A. "Das Grundproblem der Metaphysik." In *Philoso-phia perennis*, edited by J. von Rintelen. 2 vols. Regens-burg, 1930.

Rothacker, Erich. "Probleme der Kulturanthropologie." In *Systematische Philosophie*, edited by Nicolai Hartmann.

Scheler, Max. *Die Stellung des Menschen im Kosmos*. Darm-stadt, 1928.

Schöffler, Herbert. *Deutscher Osten im deutschen Geist: Von Martin Opitz zu Christian Wolff*. Frankfurt a.M., 1940.

Scholz, Heinrich. *Geschichte der Logik.* Berlin, 1931.

Schulemann, Günther. *Die Lehre von den Transzendentalien in der scholastischen Philosophie.* Leipzig, 1929.

Sertillanges, A. D. *Der heilige Thomas von Aquin.* Translated by Robert Grosche. Hellerau, 1928.

Söhngen, Gottlieb. *Sein und Gegenstand: Das scholastische Axiom "ens et verum convertuntur" als Fundament metaphysischer und theologischer Spekulation.* Münster, 1930.

Specht, Wilhelm. *Vom Wesen des Menschen: Die Grenzen seiner biologischen Erfassung.* Leipzig, 1933.

Spinoza, B. de. *Cogitata metaphysica: Opera quae supersunt omnia.* Vol. 1. Leipzig 1843.

Steinbüchel, T., and T. Müncker, eds. *Das Bild vom Menschen.* Düsseldorf, 1934.

Stöckl, Albert. *Geschichte der Philosophie des Mittelalters.* 3 vols. Mainz, 1864–66.

Suarez, Francisco. *Metaphysicae Disputationes.* Opera omnia, vols. 22–23. Moguntiae, 1605.

Thomasius, Jakob. *Erotemata metaphysica pro incipientibus.* 3d ed. Leipzig, 1692.

Thomas Aquinas. *Des hl. Thomas von Aquin Untersuchungen über die Wahrheit (Quaestiones disputatae de veritate).* Translated by Edith Stein. 2 vols. Breslau, 1931–32.

———. *In Evangelia S. Matthaei et S. Joannis Commentaria.* Turin, 1919.

———. *In Metaphysicam Aristotelis Commentaria.* Turin, 1926.

———. *Opuscula selecta.* 4 vols. Paris: Lethielleux, no year.

———. *Quaestiones disputatae et quaestiones XII quodlibetales.* 5 vols. Turin, 1924.

———. *Die Seele: Erklärungen zu den Drei Büchern des Aristoteles 'Über die Seele'.* Translated and introduced by Alois Mager. Wien, 1937.

———. *Summa contra Gentiles.* Turin, 1925.

———. *Summa theologica.* 6 vols. Turin, 1922.

Trier, Jost. *Das sprachliche Feld.* Neue Jahrbücher für Wissenschaft und Jugendbildung 10 (1934).

———. *First: Über die Stellung des Zauns im Denken der Vorzeit.* Göttingen, 1940.

———. "Deutsche Bedeutungsforschung." In *Germanische Philologie.* Heidelberg, 1934.

———. *Zaun und Mannring.* Beiträge zur Geschichte der deutschen Sprache und Literatur (1942).

Überweg, Friedrich. *Grundriss der Geschichte der Philosophie.* Vol. 2: *Die patristische und scholastische Philosophie,* edited by B. Geyer. Berlin, 1928. Vol. 3, *Die Philosophie der Neuzeit bis zum Ende des XVIII. Jahrhunderts,* edited by M. Frischeisen-Köhler and W. Moog. Berlin, 1924.

Uexküll, J. von. *Die Lebenslehre.* Potsdam-Zürich, 1930.

Uexküll, J. von, and Kriszat, G. *Streifzüge durch die Umwelten von Tieren und Menschen.* Berlin, 1934.

Vasquez, Gabriel. *Commentaria ac Disputationes in primam partem S. Thomae.* Vol. 1, Ingolstadt, 1609.

Vignaux, Paul. "Der Einfluss der Antike auf die Geistesgeschichte des Mittalalters." In *Aufsätze zur Geschichte der Antike und des Christentums.* Berlin, 1937.

Vries, Joseph de. *Denken und Sein.* Freiburg im Breisgau, 1937.

Werner, Karl. *Die Scholastik des späten Mittelalters.* 4 vols. Wien, 1881–87.

Willmann, Otto. *Geschichte des Idealismus.* 2d ed. 4 vols. Braunschweig, 1907.

Wolff, Christian. *Philosophia prima sive Ontologia: Editio nova.* Frankfurt-Leipzig, 1736.

———. *Vernünftige Gedanken von Gott, der Welt und der Seele des Menschen, auch allen Dingen überhaupt.* Frankfurt-Leipzig, 1719.

Wundt, Max. *Die deutsche Schulmetaphysik des 17. Jahrhunderts.* Tübingen, 1939.

Wuttke, H. *Christian Wolffs Lebensbeschreibung.* Leipzig, 1841.

Reality and the Good

Translated
by
Stella Lange

"A wise man is one who savors all things as they really are."

Bernard of Clairvaux

"In our doing and acting everything depends on this, that we comprehend objects clearly and treat them according to their nature."

Goethe

INTRODUCTION

The Thesis

All obligation is based upon being. Reality is the foundation of ethics. The good is that which is in accord with reality.

He who wishes to know and to do the good must turn his gaze upon the objective world of being. Not upon his own "ideas", not upon his "conscience", not upon "values", not upon arbitrarily established "ideals" and "models". He must turn away from his own act and fix his eyes upon reality.

"Reality" means two things. This twofold meaning is expressed by the two Latin words *realis* and *actualis*; the one is derived from *res*—thing, the other from *actus*—action.

Res is everything that is "presented" to our sense perception or our intellectual cognition, all that has being independently of our thinking. "Real" in this sense is whatever is "opposed" to us. Here the original meaning of the word "object" is revealed and confirmed. Not-real is that which is merely thought (but its being thought is also something real); Scholastic philosophy gave it the name *ens rationis*, "a thing of thought". Reality (in the sense of *realis*) is the whole of being which is independent of thought. When Saint Thomas wishes to designate this "reality"—not its fullness of content but its objectivity, which is antecedent to all cognition—then he uses the word *res* (which Theodor Haecker calls a "core word of Latin language" which "the Romans gave to the whole world").

The second sense of "reality" indicates the contrast not to what is merely thought but to what is merely potential—though this potentiality is also "real". The *ens in actu* is opposed not to the *ens rationis* but to the *ens in potentia*. Reality in this sense means the realized potentiality.

The statement that reality is the basis of the good is quite applicable to both meanings of "real". But in our subsequent discussion it shall be considered primarily and for the most part from the point of view of the first meaning.

According to the second and equally important meaning, the statement would signify this: to be good means to be directed toward realization. This direction toward realization must be understood primarily as the will to self-realization: "Every being is perfect insofar as it is realized, and imperfection lies in this, that its potentiality is not realized."[1]

But to be directed toward realization means also to be directed in accordance with the inherent direction of the potentiality of all things; it means an affirmation of all created being, "love" for all that is; it means desiring for and granting to every being its peculiar form of realization. All this must be thought of as completely free from any philanthropic self-complacent sentimentality. But ultimately and primarily this affirmative direction toward realization includes the direction toward God himself, who is the *Ens Actualissimum*, that being which is absolutely realized from the very beginning, in which all potentiality is completely realized in action. The affirmation of this supreme reality by man contains within itself, both as source and as summation, all modes of direction toward self-realization and all possibilities of the affirmation of that which is.[2] But this meaning of the thesis shall be touched upon only incidentally in this treatise.

Reality is the basis of the good. This means for our present purpose, according to the meaning of "real"—*realis*, that to be good is to do justice to objective being; that is good which corresponds to "the thing"; the good is that which is in accord with objective reality.

There is a statement of Goethe, "All laws and moral principles may be reduced to one—the truth."[3] But truth is the revelation of reality. Truth is the "proclamation of being",

---

[1] Unumquodque autem intantum perfectum est, inquantum est actu; nam potentia sine actu imperfecta est. *ST* I, II, 3, 2.

[2] Love of oneself is contained in the love of God. *ST* I, II, 100, 5 ad 1. Cf. *CG* 3, 22.

[3] To Müller, March 28, 1819.

says Hilary,[4] and Augustine says, "Truth is that which manifests what is."[5] So he who undertakes to reduce morality to truth, and, following this arrow, probes more deeply, beyond "truth" or rather through it, necessarily reaches being. All laws and moral principles may be reduced to reality.

The good lies indeed in the proper relation of action to the reason which truly understands, and so evil is indeed a kind of "logical" contradiction. But reason is nothing but the "passage" to reality. And he who attempts to survey at one glance this circuit—reality-understanding-action—and to express it in one word, will find that evil ultimately proves to be an "ontic" contradiction, a contradiction of being, something that opposes reality, that does not correspond to "the thing".

This makes it plain how much depends, when we are establishing a basis for ethics, on whether we start from a realistic theory of cognition or from one which—as Goethe says of Kant's—does not reach the object."[6]

An insight into the nature of the good as rooted in objective being, of itself compels us to carry it out in a definite human attitude, and it makes certain attitudes impossible.

It makes impossible the attitude of always referring to oneself and to the judgment of one's conscience, which is considered as providing the norm in each instance. We are forced now to look through and beyond our own moral judgment to the norm presented to us by the objective reality of being. When one is seeking his way, do his eyes and his glances strive for anything but this: to note the objects themselves as landmarks or hindrances and to make them yield him information? Thus, the man who wishes to realize the good does not look upon his own act but upon the truth of real objects.

"Objectivity", if thereby we mean "fidelity to being", is the proper attitude of man.

[4] Quoted *Ver.* I, I.
[5] *De vera religione* 36; quoted *Ver.* I, I.
[6] To Schultz, Sept. 18, 1831.

But we must note that man himself of course also belongs to the "objective reality of being", as an object to himself.

In the preceding pages we have formulated in outline the thesis which shall be explained and established in what follows. The explanation will be based upon the work of Saint Thomas Aquinas. However, we scarcely need to say that the purpose of this reliance upon the great doctor of the Church in our comments and explanations is not "historical".

A Realistic Theory of Cognition
and Intellectualistic Ethics

The correctness of our thesis depends on two conditions: first, the condition that our cognition attains the truth of real things, that it "reaches the object". "The cognitive spirit advances into the essence of the thing."[1] Second, the condition that our willing and acting are determined by knowledge: "The will is not the first norm; it is guided by knowledge; not only in us, but also in God."[2] Before and above the will stands the cognitive relation to reality. The good is essentially dependent upon and interiorly penetrated by knowledge. This is always and everywhere valid, even in the case of the so-called purely "voluntaristic" action, even for willing which is objectively evil. Even the man who denies that our willing and acting are determined by knowledge is in his action dependent upon that which he thinks he knows; and all evil rests in some way upon an error, upon a supposed knowledge.[3] He is good "who does the truth" (Jn 3:21). "The good, then, presupposes the true."[4] "The good, as truth, is related more primarily to knowledge than it is related, as good, to the will."[5] Virtue is "the seal of the cognitive power impressed upon the will".[6] The cognitive power is "the root of all virtue".[7] In one word:

---

[1] Intellectus penetrat usque ad rei essentiam; obiectum enim intellectus est "quod quid est." *ST* I, II, 31, 5. Omnis cognitio terminatur ad existens. *Col.* I, 4. Intellectus humani, qui est coniunctus corpori, proprium obiectum est quidditas sive natura in materia corporali existens. *ST* I, 84, 7.

[2] Voluntas non habet rationem primae regulae; . . . dirigitur enim per rationem et intellectum, non solum in nobis sed et in Deo. *Ver.* 23, 6.

[3] Cf. V. Cathrein, "Whether in every sin there is error or ignorance." Gregorianum XI (1930), 553ff.

[4] Bonum praesupponit verum. *Ver.* 21, 3.

[5] Bonum per prius pertinet ad rationem sub ratione veri quam ad voluntatem sub ratione appetibilis. *ST* I, II, 19, 3 ad 1.

[6] Virtus moralis nihil aliud est quam dispositio quaedam seu forma sigillata et impressa in vi appetitiva a ratione. *Virt. comm.* 9.

[7] Ratio est radix omnium virtutum. *Virt. comm.* 4 ad 3.

"The good of man lies in being according to reason, his evil in being against reason."[8]

The possibility of contemporary misunderstanding in regard to this ethical "intellectualism" compels us to certain explanations.

First of all, we must not overlook the fact that "reason" here not only includes but means the essential relation to reality. It is nothing else than the power of man to take into himself the truth of real things. The original meaning of the German word for reason (*Vernunft*—perception)[9] here keeps its full force, and "reason"—perception—here signifies "that which is perceived".

Furthermore, the intellectualism of Saint Thomas Aquinas—and of all Christian philosophy—must not be understood to mean that the whole realm of human action is, or can be, made clear by the light of mere human knowledge. This complete clarification is not even a true human aim or end, since in itself it transcends the power of a created spirit; man cannot know himself completely because he is not his own cause. "The first act of the will does not result from the command of reason";[10] the roots and origins of the human will do not lie in the bright field of man's own knowledge, but in the dark zone of instinctive urges or of a higher power.[11] Of course this darkness is not wholly impenetrable, but it is so for man; the "irrational" source of the human will is illumined by the divine knowledge. However, its light is "unapproachable" for the creature (1 Tim 6:16). Nevertheless, with regard

---

[8] Bonum hominis est "secundum rationem esse", malum est quod est "praeter rationem". *ST* I, II, 18, 5.

[9] We might compare here the use of the word "sensible" for "reasonable" in common English parlance. —TRANS.

[10] Primus autem voluntatis actus ex rationis ordinatione non est, sed ex instinctu naturae aut superioris causae. *ST* I, II, 17, 5 ad 3.

[11] Ibid. Also, we must, of neccesity, suppose that the will advanced to its first movement in virtue of the instigation of some exterior mover. *ST* I, II, 9, 4; cf. also *ST* I, II, 9, 6.

to the sphere of free and responsible action, it remains true: The good for man lies in being in accord with reason.[12]

This combination of a realistic theory of cognition and an "intellectualistic" ethics is the basis of all arguments for the thesis that the good is that which is in accord with reality. It is also the basis for the organization of the developing proof of this thesis. Part 1 will deal with the manner in which knowledge is related to the objective reality of being, Part 2 with the way in which the will is molded by the cognition of reality.

[12] Cf. for this J. Pieper, *Prudence* (New York: Pantheon, 1959).

PART ONE

Chapter One

Reality as the Measure of Cognition

A basic principle of any realist epistemology is this: "Objects are the measure of our knowledge."[1] Measure here does not mean something quantitative. It has nothing to do with "measuring" in the ordinary sense of the word, nor with the ethical concept of "proper measure". "Measure" as an ontological concept means something qualitative, something belonging to the realm of form and substance. Moreover, the concept of measure includes a kind of causality.[2] This meaning can still be seen in our concept of the "standard".

The concept of measure is represented and actualized in three realms of reality or, rather, three relations of reality: the relation of God and creature, the relation of the artist to his work and the relation between the objective world of being and human knowledge.

The inherent nature of something real is that which causes it to be what it is. But every created reality is not only what it is through its inherent nature. Every created reality is related to a creator who brought it into existence and formed it and through whom it is what it is. To speak more exactly, every created reality is what it is—apart from its inherent nature and anterior to it—through its relation to a creative knowledge, a creative intelligence.[3] Through the creative will a reality

[1] Ipsae res sunt causa et mensura scientiae nostrae. *Pot.* 7, 10 ad 5. Since the speculative intellect is receptive in regard to things, it is in a certain sense moved by things and consequently measured by them. *Ver.* I, 2.

[2] Compare the passages quoted under 1. Also: Our intellect receives knowledge from things, and therefore the cause and measure of truth is the being of the thing itself. *Rom.* 3, 1.

[3] Therefore, all created things are compared to God as products of art to the craftsman. But the craftsman brings his handiwork into being by the ordering of his wisdom and intellect. Therefore, God also made all creatures by the ordering of His intellect. C.G. 2, 24. God made the creature as an agent by intellect and not by a necessity of His nature. *CG* 2, 45. Cf. also *CG* 2, 46 and *ST* I, 17, 1.

possesses its existence, the fact *that* it is; through the creative knowledge a reality possesses its quality, *what* it is.[4] (The concepts "what", "nature", "true" pertain to knowledge; the concepts "that", "existence", "good" pertain to the will.) The creative intellect, of God or of the human artist, forms within itself a pattern of the reality to be created; it "pre-forms" within itself the form or nature of the reality. And because of this pre-forming, creative knowledge, the intellect or, rather, the pattern which has been formed in it becomes the "measure" of the reality.

The concept of measure must be understood through the concept of form or nature. The measure of a reality is its "external" form. It is, as Meister Eckhart said, the "preceding image". The measure is, in a very precise sense, the "model" of the reality. The inherent form of a reality is, as Scholastic philosophy expresses it, its "interior formal cause". The measure of a reality is its "exterior formal cause", through which, as well as through the interior formal cause and anterior to this, it is what it is.

The statement of Saint Thomas, *"Deus omnium entium est mensura"*, that is, God is the measure of all things,[5] means simply this: through the creative knowledge of God all real things are what they are; the divine knowledge is their exterior formal cause; all created things have their pre-form, their model, in the intellect of God; the interior forms of all reality exist as "ideas", as "preceding images" in God.

And similarly the statement that the artist is the measure of his work[6] means: the work is pre-formed in the creative knowledge of the artist; in this there exists the model of the

---

[4] Even in us the cause of one and the same effect is knowledge as directing it, whereby the form of the work is conceived, and will as commanding it, since the form as it is in the intellect only is not determined to exist or not to exist in the effect, except by the will. *ST* I, 19, 4 ad 4.

[5] *CG* 2, 12.

[6] *Ver.* I, 8.

work. The idea that has taken form in the creative knowledge of the artist is the "exterior" form of the work, through which it is what it is.

The relation of the "exterior formal cause" exists also between objective being and the intellect of man, whose cognition—as a perception of reality—is not creative but receptive. The realization of the intellect in the act, the "that" of cognition, proceeds from the spontaneous power of the subject; and this spontaneity of the mind, which in the order of being surpasses every nonrational creature, must not be "objectivistically" underrated. But the "what" of cognition stems only from the object. The object, the reality, the thing—these are the "exterior" form of the intellect, through which it is "what" it is.

> Created things, from which our intellect receives knowledge, give the measure to our intellect. But they have received their measure from the divine intellect, in which all created things are as all objects of art are in the mind of the artist. Thus, the divine intellect gives the measure and does not receive the measure. But created things both give and receive the measure. But our intellect, in regard to natural objects, is receptive of the measure and does not give the measure. It does this only in regard to artifacts.[7]

The statement that objective reality is the measure of our knowledge means precisely this: the real objects are the pre-forms and models of that which our mind cognitively forms and actually is. The world of knowledge is "pre-formed" in the objective world of being; the latter is the original image, the former the copy. The intellect "in act" is of its nature an imitation; it has an essential relation to something anterior in

---

[7] Res naturales, ex quibus intellectus noster scientiam accipit, mensurant intellectum nostrum, sed sunt mensuratae ab intellectu divino, in quo sunt omnia creata sicut omnia artificiata in intellectu artificis. Sic ergo intellectus divinus est mensurans, non mensuratus; res autem naturalis mensurans et mensurata; sed intellectus noster est mensuratus, non mensurans quidem res naturales, sed artificiales tantum. *Ver.* I, 2.

its nature. This something which naturally precedes all cognition is reality. The intellect is not "of itself"; it is something secondary and essentially dependent. "The intellect receives its measure from objects; that is, human knowledge is true not of itself, but it is true because and insofar as it conforms to reality."[8]

At first sight it seems rather unfitting that objects should be the models determining the "what" of our knowledge as the creative knowledge of God bestows the "what" upon objects. We may remark that such analogies and examples are not intended or able to bridge the abyss of the *analogia entis,* which, moreover, like the sea, is both abyss and bridge. Saint Thomas, again, who thought and wrote most profoundly about the transcendence of God over all created power, does not hesitate to say: "God is the measure of all that is; he is, therefore, related to all other beings as the objects of knowledge are related to our knowledge and constitute its measure."[9]

But that which provides the measure, the *mensura,* and that which receives the measure, the *mensuratum,* are identical in their "what".

The interior essential form of the creature, insofar as it is really itself, is in its "what" no different from the "exterior" idea of the creative intelligence of God. The work of art, insofar as it has really "emerged" into visible reality, is essentially identical with its original model in the mind of the artist; and the "what" of our knowledge, insofar as it is true, is identical with the original "what" of real objects, which are the measure of knowledge. But we certainly must not overlook the qualifying statement "insofar as it is true".

---

[8] Intellectus enim humanus est mensuratus a rebus, ut scilicet conceptus hominis non sit verus propter seipsum, sed dicitur verus ex hoc quod consonat rebus. *ST* I, II, 93, 1 ad 3.

[9] Deus omnium entium est mensura; comparatur igitur Deus ad alia entia, sicut scibile ad scientiam nostram, quod eius mensura est. *CG* 2, 12.

Mensura and *mensuratum,* that which provides the measure and that which receives the measure, differ only in their different positions in the order of importance and meaning involved in their realization. That which provides the measure is, in its quality of model and original form, identical with the recipient of the measure. That which receives the measure is, in its quality of image and copy, the very measure itself.

Our knowledge, then, as image and copy, is reality itself.

Chapter Two

The Identity of Mind and Reality

The same thing is expressed by another fundamental principle of the realist epistemology; it differs from the first one, which is more dynamic, in having a more static character. This second fundamental principle is expressed as follows: in knowledge the intellect and the known reality become one;[1] "the intellect is wholly—that is, in a perfect manner, the known object";[2] "the soul becomes, so to speak, transformed into the real object";[3] the act of knowledge brings about identity between the mind and reality.[4]

The statements we have quoted, all of which are taken from the work of Saint Thomas Aquinas, have become so strange to us that we consider it quite self-evident that they are meant to be taken only in a figurative way. Even many a Thomist takes refuge in vague limitations and restrictions, maintaining that of course there is no question of a "real" and "actual" identity here. The "naive" epistemology of the Middle Ages

---

[1] Intellectus in actu et intellectum in actu sunt unum. *CG* 2, 59.

[2] Intellectus secundum actum est omnino, id est perfecte, res intellecta. Quod quidem intelligendum est, non quod essentia intellectus fiat res intellecta vel species eius; sed quia complete informatur per speciem rei intellectae, dum eam actu intelligit. *Quol.* 7, 2.

[3] Anima quasi transformata est in rem per speciem. *Nat. verb. int.*

[4] Sciendum est ergo quod in omni intellectu aliqualiter est idem intelligens et intellectum, et in quibusdam aliqualiter differt; in aliqualibus sunt omnino idem. Intellectus enim humanus, qui aliquando est in potentia et aliquando in actu, quando est in potentia intelligens, non est idem cum intelligibili in potentia, quod est aliqua res existens extra animam; sed ad hoc quod sit intelligens in actu oportet quod intelligibile in potentia fiat intelligibile in actu per hoc quod species eius denudatur ab omnibus appendiciis materiae per virtutem intellectus agentis; et oportet quod haec species, quae est intellecta in actu, perficiat intellectum in potentia: ex quorum coniunctione efficitur unum perfectum, quod est intellectus in actu, sicut ex anima et corpore efficitur unum, quod est homo habens operationes humanas. Unde sicut anima non est aliud ab homine, ita intellectum in actu non est aliud ab intellectu intelligente actu, sed idem; non tamen ita, quod species illa fiat substantia intellectus vel pars eius, nisi formalis, sicut nec anima fit corpus. *Sen.* I, d. 35, I, 1 ad 3.

seems to us moderns, if not absurd, at least excessively and unduly simplified, and we indulge in the consideration that between Saint Thomas and ourselves there intervenes the *Critique of Pure Reason*. But we must not forget that even the mature Goethe, who like ourselves belongs to the post-Kantian age, said that what we express about objects constitutes "the real objects in our conception".[5] A few years before his death (1829), he wrote in his *Maxims and Reflections:* "There is a delicate empiricism which identifies itself intimately with the object and thereby becomes an actual experience."[6]

The identity between the intellect and the object, a true and actual self-sameness, is brought about by the immaterial, spiritual image of reality which impresses itself upon the intellect, as the seal impresses itself upon the wax. "The intellect is the known reality through the intelligible image of the reality."[7] In the image, the supermaterial core of "what-ness" of the real, formed by the creative intellect and adapted to cognition on the part of the created intellect, presents itself. It is the proper task of the spontaneous power of our mind (called *intellectus agens* by Saint Thomas[8]), which shares in and resembles the original divine spontaneity, to free this supermaterial core of "what-ness" in the real object from its material limitations. And in this illumination of sense data by the *intellectus agens,* the essentially spiritual cognition, accessible only to the immaterial "what-ness", is prepared and made possible, as the reality is raised to the state of immediate knowability.

The intelligible image, then, is on the one hand a representation of reality; indeed, in the "what" it is identical with the objective reality. "The intelligible image is in a certain sense the essence and nature of the reality itself, not according to

[5] "What we assert of things cannot be a mere notion; it is the real things in our imagination." To Riemer, Aug. 2, 1807.

[6] Number 1017 (edition Günthur Müller).

[7] Intellectus in actu est intellectum in actu propter similitudinem rei intellectae, quae est forma intellectus in actu. *ST* I, 87, 1 ad 3.

[8] *ST* I, 79, 3; 4.

natural being, but according to intelligible being."[9] But "natural being" and "intelligible being" are two ways of being, so to speak, of the same reality. They are related to each other as are the concepts "true" and "being"; and truth, if the term is used not of the judgment but of the reality itself, means nothing else than the quality of being knowable.[10] The "intelligible" being of an object is the "natural" being of the same thing, insofar as this thing is true, that is, knowable. Truth and being are really identical; "the true in objects is essentially the same as being."[11]

The reason why all these statements approach the borders of the tautological is that we are here dealing with matters that are primary and self-evident in the most literal sense and which in every effort to explain them become repetitious and trite. "The intelligible image, then, through which the reality is known, is necessarily the essence of the reality itself."[12]

On the other hand, the intelligible image which is impressed upon the intellect becomes the interior essential form of the cognitive power, which is raised to "act" through this formation; that is, which realizes its potentiality. Before the intellect is "in act", it is, Aristotle says in his book on the soul,[13] "nothing in regard to reality". And Saint Thomas says, "The potential capacity of our intellect has the same place in the order of cognition that prime matter has in the order of natural objects."[14] This means that our intellect, like prime matter at the beginning of creation, is a substantial potentiality of being, a pure possibility, receptive of being, not yet qual-

[9] Species intelligibilis est similitudo ipsius essentiae rei et est quodammodo ipsa quidditas et natura rei secundum esse intelligibile, non secundum esse naturale, prout est in rebus. *Quol.* 8, 4.

[10] Cf. *Ver.* I, I.

[11] Verum quod est in rebus, convertitur cum ente secundum substantiam. *ST* I, 16, 3.

[12] Oportet . . . speciem, qua videnda est res, esse "quod quid est" ipsius rei. Caiet. in *ST* I, 12, 2.

[13] Book III, 429 a.

[14] Intellectus autem noster possibilis se habet in ordine intelligibilium sicut materia prima in ordine rerum naturalium. *ST* I, 14, 2 ad 3.

itatively or quantitatively determined, but awaiting determination and formation, until. it rises to the point of self-realization by means of the intellectual images of the real.

Before this transformation, and only then, is the intellect in a condition of nonidentity with reality. In the measure of its self-realization it also realizes its identity with the objective world of being.[15]

The statement that the intellectual image is the interior essential form of the intellect "in act" can be completely understood only if we remember that "interior essential form" means simply that by which something is what it is. "As the soul is not something different from the man", so the intellectual image is "not something different from the intellect, but the same thing".[16] The intellectual image and the intellect are identical; it is the identity of the interior essential form of a reality with this reality itself. Indeed, the intellect and the transforming and realizing intellectual image of a reality are in a higher sense and to a greater degree identical than the potentiality of knowing before cognition and "in the act" of cognition is identical with itself. "The concept has a closer relationship to the reality conceived than it has to the one conceiving it, although the concept dwells in the one conceiving it, who is its bearer."[17] "Through the intellectual image, which is the interior essential form of the intellect, the intellect is the reality itself."[18]

The superior general of the Dominicans, Franciscus Sylvestris (Ferrariensis), in his famous commentary on the *Summa contra Gentiles,* carried on this idea as follows:

[15] It follows that sense or intellect is distinct from the sensible or intelligible object, because both are in potentiality. *ST* I, 14, 2.

[16] Compare the quotation from the commentary on the *Sententiae* under 4; it is clear from the context that here *intellectum in actu* means *species intelligibilis.*

[17] Verbum cum re dicta per verbum convenientiam habet maiorem in natura sua quam cum dicente, licet in dicente sit sicut in subiecto. *Nat. verb. int.*

[18] *ST* I, 87, 1 ad 3. Also, it is in this sense that we say that the thing actually understood is the intellect in act, because the likeness of the thing understood is the form of the intellect. *ST* I, 85, 2 ad 1.

The nature and perfection of being of the reality which exists in the objective world of being are taken up into the intellect; they bring it to the perfection of being. But because every being is what it is by virtue of its interior form, it follows that the intelligence in act is the known reality itself. For it knows in act because and insofar as the interior form of the known reality is within it. He who knows a stone is a stone, for all that possesses the interior form of a stone is a stone. However, we cannot say that the intellect which knows a stone is simply and absolutely a stone, for the essential form of the stone exists in the intellect in an intelligible way and not in its natural existence. Hence, the intellect which knows a stone is a stone in an intelligible way. The intelligence, then, which is transformed by the intelligible image of a reality can be called the reality itself because it possesses the form by which the reality is what it is.[19]

The "what" of our intellect in act is identical with the "what" of the reality upon which it is fixed in knowing. At the same time this reality of course remains in its concrete and natural "that", in its existence, really separate and different from the concrete and natural "that" of the act of knowing and of the knower himself. The known reality in our intellect ("as" something unknown) and the real object existing in objective reality are identical in their essence; they are different in the manner of being of this "what" in their existence.

The nature of knowledge lies in this relationship of essential identity and existential difference. The attempt to clarify com-

[19] Ipsa natura ut existens perfectio rei existentis extra intellectum, recipitur in intellectu, ut est de mente S. Thomae. *Ver.* 2, 2; propter quod dicitur, quod talis natura, puta lapis, perficit intellectum. Quia autem unumquodque est id, quod est, per suam formam et naturam, ideo sequitur, quod intellectus in actu, ut habet formam et naturam rei intellectae, sit ipsa res intellecta; intelligens enim lapidem est lapis, sicut et habens in se formam lapidis est lapis. Sed tamen, quia forma lapidis non habet esse naturale in intellectu, ex quo habet aliquid, ut absolute dicatur lapis, sed esse intelligibile, intellectus in actu respectu lapidis non dicitur absolute lapis, sed est lapis intelligibiliter. Hic ergo est modus quo intellectus informatus specie alicuius intellecti dicitur ipsum intellectum: quia videlicet habet formam eius per quam est tale. Ferrar. in *CG* I, 44.

pletely this relation of the two equally real situations, the attainment of reality and the separateness of consciousness, necessarily leads us to the limits of knowledge. A recognition of the mysterious character of knowledge is "the true result of a critique of knowledge".[20]

---

[20] Erich Przywara, *Ringen der Gegenwart* (Augsburg, 1929), vol. I, 263.

Chapter Three

Knowledge and Truth

The relation of the mind and objective reality to each other has three names: regarded from the point of view of the mind it is called "cognition"; regarded from the point of view of reality it is called "being known"; regarded from the point of view of both together it is called "truth".

"Intelligent beings are distinguished from nonintelligent beings in this way, that the nonintelligent have no form but their own; but the intelligent being is capable of having also the form of another being. That is why the philosopher says that the soul is in a certain manner all things."[1]

To *have* a form means to be something definite. Everything is what it is through the form which it has. To know, then, means to have the forms of other things, to be the other, to be identical with the other, to be all things. "That is why the philosopher says that the soul *is* all things." To know is to become another.[2]

We must distinguish between the process of cognition and knowledge as an accomplished fact. The process of cognition is both active and passive. Actively it is the separation of the supermaterial, intelligible core of being of the objects from the sensible shell of matter, a spontaneous penetration into the realm of immaterial essentiality through which the intellect really comes to the active realization of its own self. Passively it consists of the admission, the reception, of the essential form of the reality.

---

[1] Cognoscentia a non cognoscentibus in hoc distinguuntur, quia non cognoscentia nihil habent nisi formam suam tantum; sed cognoscens natum est habere formam etiam rei alterius. Nam species cogniti est in cognoscente. Unde manifestum est quod natura rei non cognoscentis est magis coarctata et limitata. Natura autem rerum cognoscentium habet maiorem amplitudinem et extensionem. Propter quod dicit Philosophus, quod anima est quodammodo omnia. *ST* I, 14, 1; cf. also *ST* I, 80, 1 and *Ver.* 2, 2.

[2] Sertillanges, *St. Thomas d' Aquin* (Paris, 1910), vol. 2, 105.

This active-passive process is unessential in regard to knowledge as an accomplished fact; or rather, this activity and passivity is necessary for knowledge to come about, but it does not constitute the essence of actual knowledge.[3] The essence of knowledge is the *possession* of the forms of objective reality; knowledge as an accomplished fact is not an "activity" of the intellect but its realization. It is the relation of the mind to objective reality. It is the identity between the knowing soul and the reality, regarded from the point of view of the knowing soul, which in this identity realizes its own potentiality.[4]

It is this very relation of the intellect and the reality which constitutes the conceptual content of "truth". Truth is the conformity *(conformitas)* and the assimilation *(adaequatio)* — taking both terms in their most exact sense — of reality and knowledge. And this relation is realized in the very act of knowledge: "In the operation of the intellect there is accomplished the relation of assimilation in which lies the essence of truth."[5] Truth is nothing else than the relation of identity between the mind and the reality, a relation consisting in and accomplished in knowledge, and in this relation the reality is the measure of the intellect.

---

[3] Intellectus non se habet ut agens vel ut patiens, nisi per accidens; inquantum scilicet ad hoc quod intelligibile uniatur intellectui, requiritur actio vel passio; actio quidem secundum quod intellectus agens facit species esse intelligibilis actu; passio autem secundum quod intellectus possibilis recipit species intelligibiles. . . . Sed hoc quod est intelligere, consequitur ad hanc passionem vel actionem sicut effectus ad causam. *Ver.* 8, 6.

[4] . . . only if there is something which is such that it agrees with every being. Such a being is the soul, which as is said in *The Soul* "in some way is all things". *Ver.* I, 1.

[5] In ipsa operatione intellectus . . . completur relatio adaequationis, in qua consistit ratio veritatis. *Sen.* I, d. 19, 5, 1.

Chapter Four

Objectivity as an Attitude in Knowing

The nature of knowledge rests upon objectivity as the only proper attitude of man. (Objectivity as an ethical attitude in a narrower sense shall be discussed in Part 2.) If we demand objectivity in knowing, this means simply that knowledge must be really knowledge. Nothing else is involved here but the true character of knowledge.

Knowledge is the relation between the subject and the object, determined in its "that" by the subject, in its "what" by the object. So the activity and the influence of the subject upon knowledge is—insofar as real, that is, true, knowledge is concerned—confined to the positing of its existence. The content, the "what", the nature of the knowledge, is determined solely by the matter, the thing, the object—insofar as we are dealing with true knowledge. If, then, any determination of the content by the will of the subject enters into the knowledge, if the subject wishes one thing to be so, something to be different and something else not to be at all; then, as far as this personal subjective influence extends, there is actually no knowledge at all.

This does not mean that ultimate passivity is the proper attitude in regard to knowledge or the suitable attitude for man in general. First of all, a tremendous activity of the will is required if we are to be determined only by reality in our knowing, to be objective and to force ourselves to silence and keep ourselves out of the picture and so to become perceptive. We are beginning to understand once more the meaning of objectivity in perception, to recognize that there can and must be a kind of asceticism of knowledge.

Secondly, the spontaneously moving penetration by the mind of the intellectually knowable nature of reality, which prepares for the actual knowing, is really a supreme activity. Of this we have already spoken.

Moreover, thirdly, there is a place for the individual view of the subject, which differs in regard to the content of knowledge, if only because of the variety of the objective reality, which appears to different persons in different ways, but to each one as it really is.

Finally, the will of the subject and his affirmative or negative or indifferent attitude toward the object will, of course, definitely determine the intensity and the direction of his attention and awareness. But this influence of the subject does not affect the "what" of knowledge, but only its "that", the setting up and carrying out of the "objective" of knowledge.[1]

Another argument basic for objectivity lies in the order of the objects of knowledge, which is in a certain sense a hierarchy. Here we can deal with this only summarily.

The human intellect first knows the objective being presented to it, thereafter the act of knowing, the faculty of knowing and the knowing subject itself as subject.[2] That —and in what sense—this order, in which the object precedes the subject, is also a hierarchy may be seen in the following statements of Saint Thomas: "Nobody knows that he knows except by the fact that he knows something; for knowing something precedes one's knowing oneself as knowing." "Our intellect cannot know itself by being immediately aware of itself; but by being aware of something else it comes to know itself."[3]

---

[1] Cf. J. Pieper, "*Wirklichkeitswissenschaftliche" Soziologie. Kritische Randbemerkungen zu Hans Freyer, "Soziologie als Wirklichkeitswissenschaft."* Archiv für Sozialwissenschaft und Sozialpolitik, vol. 66, 394–407.

[2] Cf. *Ver.* 10, 8 and *ST* I, 87, 3.

[3] Nullus percipit se intelligere nisi ex hoc quod aliquid intelligit: quia prius est intelligere aliquid quam intelligere se intelligere. . . . Intellectus . . . non est intelligibilis nisi per speciem superinductam. . . . Mens nostra non potest seipsum intelligere ita, quod seipsam immediate apprehendat; sed ex hoc quod apprehendit alia, devenit in suam cognitionem. *Ver.* 10, 8.

That means, the intellect itself becomes knowable only when it has taken into itself the essential form of an objective reality, for it is only in this way that it attains true self-realization, and a thing is knowable only in the measure in which it is real. Only through the entrance of objective reality into our being do we reach our true selfhood. Only on the basis of and by means of knowledge of the objective world of being does the intellect enter the realm of that which can be its own object. Goethe says: "A man knows himself only insofar as he knows the world."

PART TWO

Chapter Five

The Unity of Theoretical and Practical Reason

Human reason, by realizing itself through knowledge, refers back to the objective world of being upon which it is dependent, by which it is interiorly formed and with which it is identical. To this basic statement of realist epistemology Christian occidental philosophy adds as "intellectualistic" ethics the statement: the free moral action of man refers back to the reason, upon which it is dependent and by which it is interiorly formed.

To clarify the relation between these two theses we must first make some distinctions.

First of all, we must not overlook the fact that in these statements the word "reason" has two meanings. In the first statement it means the theoretical, speculative reason, in the second the practical reason. Reason is "theoretical" when it is turned receptively toward the real objects presented to it. Reason is practical when it turns toward acting *(agere)* and making *(facere)*.

Thus, the chain by which the good is bound to reality is composed of the following links: objective reality, theoretical reason, practical reason, moral action. After showing that, and how, the first two links are connected, and before speaking of the connection of the last two, we must grasp the relation of the theoretical and the practical reason.

Theoretical reason itself becomes "in extending", *per extensioneum,* the practical reason. [1] "The practical reason, like the speculative, knows the truth, but it orders the known truth toward action"; [2] through the extension of knowledge toward willing and acting, the theoretical reason becomes practical.

---

[1] *ST* I, 79, 11, sed contra.
[2] Intellectus enim practicus veritatem cognoscit sicut speculativus, sed veritatem cognitam ordinat ad opus. *ST* I, 79, 11 ad 2.

This means first of all that the theoretical and the practical reason are not two distinct powers of the soul.[3] Nor are they two separate and independent operations of one and the same "basic faculty". This is how Kant seems to understand the relation of the theoretical and the practical reason. He speaks of a "common principle" of both[4] and of the "speculative use of reason" and of the "practical use of reason".[5] In spite of their being rooted in a single theoretical-practical "basic faculty", Kant makes the practical reason entirely independent of the theoretical and of all that can be the object of theoretical activity, that means, independent of all knowledge of reality.

Moreover, this is not a harmless unessential speculation for philosophers. In making the practical reason—that is, the power of the soul that determines action—independent of the theoretical reason—that is, the power of the soul that perceives objective being—Kant sees, according to Richard Kroner, nothing less than "the conquest of the metaphysics of being, the transfer of the center of gravity from the object to the subject".[6] Therefore, our examination of reality and the good might be quite correct in considering the unity of the theoretical and the practical reason, and the priority of the theoretical reason upon which this unity is based, to be precisely the ontological foundation of ethics and the starting point for a transfer of the center of gravity from the subject back to the object, to objective reality.

The concept of the practical reason necessarily includes and asserts the theoretical reason as well. The "basic faculty" is the

[3] The speculative and practical intellects are not distinct powers. The reason of which is that what is accidental to the nature of the object of a power does not differentiate that power. . . . Now, to a thing apprehended by the intellect, it is accidental whether it be directed to operation or not, and according to this the speculative and practical intellects differ. For it is the speculative intellect which directs what it apprehends, not to operation, but to the consideration of truth; while the practical intellect is that which directs what it apprehends to operation. *ST* I, 79, 11.

[4] *Grundlegung zur Metaphysik der Sitten*, Introduction.

[5] Ibid, Conclusion.

[6] Richard Kroner, *Von Kant zu Hegel* (Tübingen, 1921/24), vol. I, 153.

theoretical reason, which "extends" to become the practical. The theoretical includes the practical, somewhat as the genus includes the distinct species. Only insofar as it is theoretical is the reason also practical. Prior to all action is the "theoretic" perception of reality. *Intellectus speculativus fit practicus,* the theoretic reason "becomes" practical.[7] All that is practical is rooted in the theoretical and presupposes it.

If we consider the relationship of the *object* of the theoretical reason to that of the practical reason, the result is the same. The proper object of the theoretical reason is the truth in things. The proper object of the practical reason is "the true as the measure of action",[8] "the true which extends into the good".[9] The object of the theoretical reason includes and comprises the object of the practical reason. The object of the theoretical reason, the true, "becomes" the object of the practical reason by establishing a relation with the object of the will.

The practical reason, then, is nothing but the theoretical reason itself regarded under the aspect of a special function. But we must note this: it is not quite correct to say that classical Christian philosophy maintains an actual "primacy" of the theoretical reason over the practical reason and of theory over practice in general. Primacy in the strict sense can exist only in the relationship of realities which are independent of each other. There can be primacy in the relation of Saint Peter to the other apostles, and Kant can also speak of a real primacy in the relation of the practical reason to the theoretical. But it is not possible to speak of a primacy of the foundation over the building, for the building includes the foundation. And this same relation exists between the theoretical and the practical reason.

The "extension" by which the theoretical reason becomes practical is directed, as we said, toward willing and action.

[7] *ST* I, 79, 11, sed contra.
[8] *Sen.* 3, d. 23, 2, 3, 2.
[9] *Sen.* I, d. 27, 2, 1.

This "particular function" of direction toward the will consists in the deciding, commanding, guiding causation of free action. We shall speak of this in detail.

But we can already see the outline of the situation. Reason, as practical reason, would not be turned toward willing and action if it had not previously, as theoretical reason, also been turned toward things. It could not be decisive and commanding if it were not first made accessible to being through knowledge. It would not be the measure of action if it did not first receive its measure from objective reality.

The decision to do a definite thing, which is an interior "command" *(imperium)* given to ourselves by ourselves, and which precedes a free action, does not come blindly and at random. Knowledge of being is "lengthened" and transformed into decision and command. The imperative is founded upon an indicative; the latter makes the former possible. Essentially prior to the decision and command is the purely perceptive statement. The "image" of the real precedes and underlies the "plan" of all realization.

Decision and command, in which the practical reason is realized, signify, then, a knowledge which turns toward the will. But knowledge is an essential identity of the mind with the objective reality. The relation of these two facts reveals the measure and the manner in which the practical reason proper, which on its part determines the free act, is essentially bound up with the objective reality which is perceived in our knowledge of being. This also gives us a clear view of the purpose of our task: to show in detail how, in the fact that action is determined by knowledge, action is really determined by the objective reality itself.

Chapter Six

The Structure of Moral Action

The extension of the reason, which perceives reality, toward willing and action is not begun and ended in a single act. But this turning toward the will gradually increases in intensity, moving step by step through the numerous partial acts of which moral action as a whole is composed, and so becomes the decision and command directed immediately toward action.

The partial acts of which, as we said, moral action is composed, are acts of knowledge and of will, and those of the will are so arranged that every single act of knowledge is followed by an act of will. "Because the will follows the reason, the process of the will corresponds to that of the reason."[1] In the gradation of the cognitive partial acts the self-extension of the reason toward the will is realized; in the succession of these cognitive partial acts the reason becomes practical.

It is not that in the continued succession of acts the theoretical disappears, so to speak, for it is the theoretical reason itself which becomes practical through its extension toward the will; it is the cognitive reason turned toward reality, which, as practical, gives its commands to the will.

It is indispensable at this point to give a brief, perhaps too condensed, but necessarily somewhat "academic" account of the structure of moral action.[2] (The diagram on page 179 may serve to make the account more clear.)

---

[1] *Sen.* 3, d. 17, 1, 2, 1.
[2] Saint Thomas did not present moral action from a single point of view. As far as the cognitive partial acts are concerned, he presented them in part under the aspect of the *habitus* supporting them, e.g., *synderesis* and *prudentia*; or else he takes individual partial acts and gives a detailed phenomenological description, e.g., in the case of *consilium* and *imperium; consilium, indicium* and *imperium* he combines under the concept of the virtue of prudence; the act of *synderesis* he considers both from the point of view of its supporting *habitus* and from the point of view of its content, which is the natural moral law.

The first prerequisite for effective willing is the knowledge of the end or, what amounts to the same thing, the good[3] that shall be attained or realized. "The awareness of the end must be considered the first thing in the realm of action."[4] Only through knowledge does that which is to be realized come within the range and reach of the man who acts. "The good, under the aspect of the true, has a relation to the reason that is prior to that which, under the aspect of something to be striven for, it has to the will; for the will could not turn toward the good if this had not first been grasped by the reason."[5] Seeing the good is the first and lowest level of cognitive acts in the structure of moral action.

This is followed by the first volitional act of simple "willing" *(volitio)*, the love of the good as such. "In the volitional sphere love is the prime source of any movement toward an end."[6]

The first cognitive act, the sight of the good, is purely per- ceptive, theoretical, "speculative", mirroring the reality. Hence, the order in which "simple willing follows" the sight of the good is not based upon a causality of the reason for- mally directed toward the will and in any way "imperative". The cause of the order is that the reason "presents" its object to the will.

The reason becomes practical in the proper sense, that is, deciding, commanding and directing, only at the second stage of the cognitive partial act, in the imperative voice of the pri- mordial conscience *(synderesis)*.[7] In this act of the primordial

---

[3] Bonum habet rationem finis. *ST* I, 5, 2 ad 2.

[4] In ordine autem agibilium primo quidem oportet sumere apprehen- sionem finis. *ST* I, II, 15, 3.

[5] *ST* I, II, 19, 3 ad 1.

[6] In unoquoque autem horum appetituum amor dicitur illud quod est prin- cipium motus tendentis in finem amatum. *ST* I, II, 26, 1.

[7] The curious word *synderesis* is the Greek συντέρησις [= preservation]; the Latin form can be explained by the medieval Greek pronunciation. In the translation of the *Summa Theologica* by Joseph Bernhart, *synderesis* is translated by "Gewissensurschatz" (primitive store of conscience). This rather felicitous rendering is, however, deficient in that it expresses rather the content of the primordial conscience than this conscience itself.

conscience the reason begins to be practical; here the extension
to the will begins. In the voice of the primordial conscience
moral action as such also commences. The practical insight of
the primordial conscience corresponds to the theoretical insight into the supreme basic principles of thought. The primordial conscience is the supreme awareness—transcending
and independent of all efforts of thought—of the primary, basic first principles of action,[8] summed up in the imperative: we
must love the good.[9]

In the order of the acts of the will, the imperative voice of
the primordial conscience is followed by the "striving" for
the end *(intentio finis)*. It is distinguished from the first act of
the will—the simple willing—in the same way as the act of
the primordial conscience is distinguished from the mere
sight of the good. The theoretic intelligence first sees the
good as such; the primordial conscience, in its practical
knowledge, considers the good as the motive and source of
action. Thus, the "willing" is directed to the good as such;
the "striving" considers the good as the goal of the free
movement of the willing person, that is, the end of its
action.[10]

The next action of the practical reason is "the consideration
of what is to be done", the *consilium,* taking counsel with
oneself.[11] The command of the primordial conscience and the

[8] There is in the soul a natural habit of first principles of action, which are
the universal principles of the natural law. This habit pertains to synderesis.
Ver. 16, 1.

[9] The act of the natural habit called *synderesis* is to warn against evil and to
incline to good. *Ver.* 16, 1 ad 12.

[10] The act of the will is to will, to choose and to intend. It is to will insofar
as reason proposes to the will something good absolutely. . . . It is to intend
insofar as reason proposes to the will a good as an end to be attained through
a means. *Ver.* 22, 15. Cf. also *ST* I, II, 12, 2.

[11] Sunt autem quatuor actus rationis, secundum quod dirigit humanos actus: quorum primus est intellectus quidam, quo aliquis recte existimat de fine,
qui est sicut principium in operativis. . . . Secundus actus est consilium de
agendis. *Mal.* 14, 4.

It is tempting to interpret the *recte existimare de fine*, which here appears as
the "first act" of the reason "insofar as it directs human actions", as the voice

"striving" are directed toward the end; the consideration and the following partial acts have to do with the means to the end.[12]

The consideration may lead to the conclusion that there are several appropriate means to accomplish the end. To this "intermediate" conclusion of the consideration there corresponds, on the part of the acts of will, the "consent" *(consensus)* of the will to the entirety of the appropriate means.[13]

The real final conclusion of the consideration is the "judgment"[14] that among the totality of the appropriate means *one* definite way to the end is recognized as the one to be taken rather than the others.

To this judgment the will responds by the "decision" *(electio)*.[15] This choice of the will is the actual definite willing, the decision for something concrete and therewith the exclusion of all other possibilities.[16]

If the consideration throughout reveals only one means to realize the end, then the "consent" and the "choice" coincide.[17]

The final cognitive partial act, in which the extension of the reason toward action is completed, is the "resolution" or "command" *(imperium)*, the immediate order given to the will

---

of the primordial conscience. But we must consider that *existimare* does not imply an imperative but rather a theoretical evaluation.

[12] Because counsel is an inquiry, it is not of the end but only of the means. *ST* I, II, 14, 2.

[13] The application of the appetitive movement to counsel's decision is consent properly speaking. *ST* I, II, 15, 3.

[14] All thought about those things of which counsel takes cognizance is directed to the formation of a right judgment, wherefore this thought is perfected in judgment. *ST* II, II, 53, 4 ad 2. Also: Tertius actus est iudicium de agendis. *Mal.* 15, 4. Compare the passage quoted under 11.

[15] A decision or judgment, to be followed by choice. *ST* I, II, 13, 1 ad 2.

[16] Choice is the taking of one thing in preference to another. *ST* I, II, 13, 2.

[17] Sed si inveniatur unum solum quod placeat, non differunt re consensus et electio. *ST* I, II, 15, 3 ad 3.

to "use" the chosen means.[18] In this command the reason becomes in the final and preeminent sense "practical reason". "To command is the proper function of the practical reason."[19]

The will obeys the command of the reason in arousing the powers of the person and "using" them *(usus activus)* to carry out the command. This execution is nothing but the "use" *(usus passivus)* of human powers by the will.[20]

It is probably not necessary to protect this enumeration of the steps of moral action against the naive misunderstanding that it means something more than a diagrammatic summary. This claims, however, to follow faithfully, though with some simplification, the structure of the moral activity of the will.

The actual principle of the succession of the theoretic partial acts, from the first sight of the good to the immediate concrete command given to the will, is the extension of the reason toward will and action which is realized in this process. The dependence of the will upon knowledge increases, in the succession of the partial acts, from a purely factual "following" to a real "obedience" to the reason, which in the act of "commanding" avails itself of this dependence. The causality of the reason, as directed toward the will, buds in the simple sight of the good. It works more plainly in the voice of the primordial conscience, which is a formal command, even though not very concrete. It unfolds fully and finally when the practical

---

[18] Not every act of the will precedes this act of the reason which is command; but an act of the will precedes, viz. choice, and an act of the will follows, viz. use. Because after counsel's decision, which is reason's judgment, the will chooses; and after choice the reason commands that power which has to do what was chosen, and then, last of all, someone's will comes to use, by executing the command of reason. *ST* I, II, 17, 3 ad 1.

[19] Now there are three acts of reason in respect to anything done by man: the first of these is counsel, the second judgment, the third command. . . . The third is proper to the practical intellect, insofar as this is ordained to operation. *ST* I, II, 57, 6.

[20] *ST* I, II, 16, 4.

reason takes the will into its service in the act of the concrete "command", which immediately precedes the properly executive action of the will.[21]

Another mark, also basic to the nature of this succession of partial acts of reason, is this: every succeeding act is more concrete and less general than the preceding one. The voice of the primordial conscience is directed very generally toward *the* good as the end of human action; in the "choice" the reason chooses *one* particular way to the end, whereas the "consideration" which precedes the judgment is concerned with a number of ways.

This mark of increasing particularization reflects the first sign of the increasing extension of the reason toward the will. Reason as such grasps what is general, but the will strives toward particular objects.[22]

We shall name a final mark of this succession of acts: each succeeding act has less of necessity and certainty than the preceding one. The primordial conscience is unerring.[23] Its voice "is always right"[24] and "never makes a mistake".[25] "Just as in

---

[21] The extension of the reason to include willing, which takes place in the succession of the cognitive partial acts, is however, not a simple progressive movement of the practical element in them. The practical element in the reason, in the course of the cognitive partial acts, reaches, so to speak, two climaxes, one in the voice of the primordial conscience, the other in the "command" of prudence. These two acts constitute "climaxes" of the practical element because both are imperatives. The voice of the primordial conscience is a general and abstract imperative; the "command" of prudence a definite and concrete one. The voice of the primordial conscience is preceded by the purely theoretic acts of cognition; between the voice of the primordial conscience and the concrete "command" lie the more theoretical acts of "consideration" and "judgment".

[22] Ratio apprehendit aliquid in universali, sed appetitus tendit in res quae habent esse particulare. *ST* I, II, 66, 3.

[23] *Synderesis* does not mean the rational power simply but as perfected by a completely determined habit. *Ver.* 16, 2, ad 4.

[24] As a result, for probity to be possible in human actions, there must be some permanent principle which has unwavering integrity, in reference to which all human works are examined, so that that permanent principle will resist all evil and assent to all good. This is synderesis, whose task it is to warn

the theoretical sphere the reason cannot err about the first basic principles, so it cannot be mistaken about the first basic
principles of action. Therefore, we say that the primordial
conscience is indestructible."[26] But consideration, choice and
command are by no means free from the possibility of error.

Now we must explain how in the individual partial acts the
fact that the practical reason is determined by reality is connected with its function of originating and determining
action. This explanation will be divided into two sections.
The first deals with the primordial conscience, its relation to
objective reality and its relation to will and action. The second
section sums up the remaining partial acts of the practical reason—consideration, choice, and command—under the aspect
of prudence. For the virtue of prudence is nothing else than
the art of considering, deciding and commanding rightly.[27]
Here too we shall see the determining nature of reality on the
one hand and the relation to action on the other.

---

against evil and incline to good. Therefore, we agree that there can be no error
in it. *Ver.* 16, 2.

[25] Just as in the operative part of the soul synderesis never errs, so in the
speculative part understanding of principles never errs. *Ver.* 16, 1.

[26] Sicut non contingit in speculativis intellectum errare circa cognitionem
primorum principiorum, quin semper repugnet omni ei quod contra principia
dicitur, ita etiam non contingit errare in practicis in principiis primis; et
propter hoc dicitur quod synderesis extingui non potest. *Sen.* 2, d. 39, 3, 1.

[27] Ad prudentiam pertinet recte consiliare, iudicare et praecipere de his per
quae pervenitur ad debitum finem. *ST* II, II, 47, 10.

Chapter Seven

The Voice of the Primordial Conscience

The primordial conscience is a natural, innate "attitude" *(habitus)* of the human mind by which it is destined to have a primary and infallible judgment about the good as the end and the meaning of human action. The voice of the primordial conscience is—as to its content—the natural moral law. The primordial conscience is the natural awareness of the ethical natural law.[1]

The voice of the primordial conscience is the practical basic principle, simply and absolutely, upon which the whole moral motivation of rational beings depends. "The original direction of all our actions toward the end is necessarily brought about by the natural law."[2]

The practical basic principle governs the whole sphere of the practical just as the theoretic basic principle, the law of identity, governs the whole sphere of theoretical thinking. The law of identity is based upon the concept of being; the voice of the primordial conscience is based upon the concept of the good.[3]

There are two modes of a rational judgment (and the primordial conscience definitely belongs to the sphere of

---

[1] *Synderesis* is said to be the law of our mind, because it is a habit containing the precepts of the natural law. *ST* I, II, 94, 1 ad 2. The natural law is contained primarily in the eternal law, but secondarily in the natural code of the human reason. *ST* I, II, 71, 6 ad 4. The precepts of the natural law are to the practical reason what the first principles of demonstrations are to the speculative reason. *ST* I, II, 94, 2.

[2] Oportet quod prima directio actuum nostrorum ad finem fiat per legem naturalem. *ST* I, II, 91, 2 ad 2. Also: The first rule of reason is the natural law. *ST* I, II, 95, 2. Not conscience, but synderesis is the first rule of human activity. *Ver.* 17, 2 ad 7. Natural reason, known by the name of synderesis, appoints the end to moral virtues. *ST* II, II, 47, 6 ad 1.

[3] The first principle in the practical reason is one founded on the notion of good. *ST* I, II, 94, 2.

reason[4]): the mode of the pure statement, the indicative *(modus enuntiandi)*, and the mode of command, the imperative *(modus praecipiendi)*.[5]

The fact of being based upon the concept of the good is by itself not the supreme basic principle of the practical reason; for the definition of the good, which is a purely indicative statement ("The good is that toward which everything strives"[6]), is also based upon the *concept* of the good. But it is immediately evident that the basic principle of the practical reason must be stated differently. The practical is a movement of being, governed by the mind. Hence, the basic principle of the practical must contain within itself this movement, still potential, as its cause, source and essence. But the definition of the good, although based upon the concept of the good, is purely theoretic and static. It does not have the dynamic element, the element of motion. This dynamic element is found in the other mode of the reasoned judgment, in the imperative. The structure of the imperative is: this must be that. The "must be" is the expression and the medium of motion. Therefore, in order that the indicative definition of the good may "extend" to become the practical basic principle, this "must be" must enter into it. The good must be that toward which everything strives. In other words: we must love the good, *bonum faciendum est.*[7]

---

[4] There is no act ascribed to synderesis which cannot be performed by reason. *Ver.* 16, 1. The natural law is something appointed by reason. *ST* I, II, 94, 1.

[5] Sicut enuntiatio est rationis dictamen per modum enuntiandi, ita lex per modum praecipiendi. *ST* I, II, 92, 2.

[6] Bonum est quod omnia appetunt. *Ver.* 21, 1.

[7] In itself it might be possible to take the voice of the primordial conscience, if it is considered in isolation, as a purely indicative statement: *bonum est faciendum*, the good "is" that which should be. O. Renz in his comprehensive work on synderesis in Thomas Aquinas (Münster, 1911), at least in the chapter on the "evidence" of the synderesis judgment (p. 70), almost completely disregarded its dynamic, imperative character. The judgment of the synderesis, says Renz, is "objectively evident" because in it subject and predicate are identical. But this way of looking at things is possible and meaningful only in pure indicative statements. The judgment of the synderesis, however,

Now we can formulate the practical basic principle, the voice of the primordial conscience: "The supreme principle of the practical reason is based upon the concept of the good, which is as follows: the good is that toward which everything strives. So this is the supreme statement of the law: We must do and love the good, and we must avoid the evil."[8]

The dynamic, imperative character of the primordial conscience is derived from a preliminary act of the will. All movement comes from the will. "Reason also receives its motive power from the will."[9] This act of the will which precedes the voice of the primordial conscience is the simple willing of the natural love for the good. "The order of the natural law follows the order of the natural inclinations of our being."[10] Of this we shall speak in greater detail.

The relation of the primordial conscience and its voice to the concrete moral action is brought about by the "striving" and the other partial acts, which in the diagrammatic sketch of the total moral action lie between the voice of the primordial conscience and the "carrying out" of the concrete command of the practical reason.

The relation of command and obedience is found directly in the dependence of the "striving" upon the voice of the primordial conscience. The "striving" is the answer and the immediate obedience of the will to the ethical natural law

---

is not "the good 'is' that which should be", but "the good 'should be' ". The same thing is expressed in the fact that Saint Thomas calls the content of the synderesis judgment "the natural *law*".

[8] Et ideo primum principium in ratione practica est quod fundatur supra rationem boni, quae est "bonum est quod omnia appetunt". Hoc est ergo primum praeceptum legis, quod bonum est faciendum et prosequendum, et malum vitandum. *ST* I, II, 94, 2.

[9] It follows that the very fact that the reason moves by commanding is due to the power of the will. *ST* I, II, 17, 1. A form considered by the intellect neither moves nor causes anything except through the medium of the will, whose object is an end and a good by which one is moved to act. *CG* 1, 72.

[10] Secundum ordinem inclinationum naturalium est ordo praeceptorum legis naturalis. *ST* I, II, 94, 2.

formulated in the voice of the primordial conscience: "The good must be the end of human action." The "striving" is the reply: "I *will* the good as the end of my action."[11]

The rightness of this act of will is the foundation of prudence[12] and so of the rightness of all the succeeding partial acts of the practical reason.[13] The "consideration"[14] and the "command"[15] are rooted in this act of striving for the end. It is time to call to the reader's attention that the determination of willing and action by the voice of the primordial conscience is already beginning to appear in outline.

The wholly concrete moral action of the will is entirely and immediately formed by and dependent upon the concrete "command" of the practical reason. But the concrete command of the practical reason is in a very definite way related to the earlier general voice of the primordial conscience. And this relation determines the dependence of the concrete moral action upon the primordial conscience itself.

---

[11] Intention is an act of the will in regard to the end. Now the will stands in a threefold relation to the end. First, absolutely; and thus we have volition. . . . Secondly, it considers the end as its place of rest; and thus enjoyment regards the end. Thirdly, it considers the end as the term toward which something is ordained; and thus intention regards the end. For when we speak of intending to have health, we mean not only that we will have it, but that we will have it by means of something else. *ST* I, II, 12, 1 ad 4. Intention regards the end as a terminus of the movement of the will. *ST* I, II, 12, 2.

[12] This dependence of prudence upon the will, however, is of a very different kind from the dependence of the external action of the will upon the "command" of prudence. Here it is not a matter of likeness and reciprocity. The dependence of the will upon the reason concerns the "what" of willing and action, just as the dependence of the reason upon reality concerns the "what" of thinking. But the "command" of prudence does not receive its "what" through the rightness of the will, but the rightness of the preceding act of the will makes it possible that the "command" of prudence receive its "what" from true knowledge. Therefore, P. T. Deman, O.P., is mistaken in his criticism of the first edition of this book. Cf. *Revue des sciences philosophiques et théologiques*, 19, 718ff.

[13] *ST* II, II, 47, 13 ad 2.

[14] *ST* I, II, 15, 3.

[15] *ST* I, II, 90, 1 ad 3.

In the voice of the primordial conscience ("the good must be loved"), the material and formal basic structure of all concrete "commands" of the practical reason is given, just as the material and formal basic structure of all concrete individual statements is found in the principle of identity ("that which is, is").

This statement, which expresses the dependence of the concrete "command" upon the voice of the primordial conscience, requires a brief explanation. In every judgment we distinguish between "matter" and "form". The subject and the predicate are the logical "matter"; the copula is the logical "form". In combining or dividing the subject and the predicate, it expresses a judgment about what it is. In every individual theoretical judgment—whose pattern is "this is that", the matter ("this", "that") and the form ("is")—the structure of the principle of identity recurs; the final statement that can be made about every "this" and "that" is that it is. The principle of identity states that whatever is, is. The concrete theoretical individual judgment states that *this* which is, is. Hence, the principle of identity, material and formal, is the basic structure of every concrete statement.

In the same way the voice of the primordial conscience, which is the "principle of identity" in the realm of the practical, affects all the concrete imperatives of the practical reason. The voice of the primordial conscience says: "The good, whatever it may be, must be." Every concrete "command" of the practical reason says: "*This* good must be." So the "principle of identity" of the primordial conscience is likewise the basic structure materially and formally affecting and regulating all the commands of the practical reason.

The other question, whether the primordial conscience is determined by objective reality, cannot be answered, any more than the first question, by the means provided by empirical psychology. The voice of the primordial conscience is a purely natural thing, preceding all possibility of conscious control. But the question is not really put in this way. It means this: Does the voice of the primordial conscience necessarily presuppose a definite relation to objective reality?

To this we must reply, first of all, that certainly the voice of the primordial conscience presupposes a knowledge and awareness of reality.[16] The imperative of the primordial conscience would not be possible without a preceding knowledge. It is, like every command of the practical reason, a transformed knowledge; "To command means to apply knowledge to willing and working."[17]

The imperative *form* of that voice is derived, as we have said, from a preceding act of the will. But the *content*, that which is commanded, the *matter*, comes from the theoretic reason, which is turned toward reality. The "what" of the imperative of the primordial conscience is based upon knowledge; its "that" is based upon the will. If the will were not active, no imperative could come about; the "must be" would be unthinkable. But the "must be" would be without content if, before the imperative, the intelligence had not been aware of being.

Knowledge is relation to objective reality, identity of the mind with the world of being. So it is the same thing if we say that the voice of the primordial conscience includes knowledge or if we say that it presupposes a relation to reality.

The knowledge which is included in and presupposed by the voice of the primordial conscience is the knowledge of the good. "It is peculiar to the primordial conscience to oppose the evil and to strive for the good, but it could not do this if it had not first really known the good and the evil."[18] The content and basis of the primordial conscience is the concept

---

[16] Actus cognitionis praeexigitur ad actum ipsius (synderesis). *Ver.* 16, 1 ad 14. This touches upon the fact that the primordial conscience is an innate *habitus*: an act of knowing is not prerequisite for the power or habit of synderesis, but only for its act. Hence, this does not prevent the habit of synderesis from being innate. Ibid.

[17] Praecipere quod est applicare cognitionem habitam ad appetendum et operandum *ST* II, II, 47, 16.

[18] *Ver.* 16, 1, obj. 14 ad 14.

of the good, *fundatur supra rationem boni*.[19] The knowledge of the nature of the good becomes imperative in the voice of the primordial conscience.

But knowledge of the nature of the good necessarily includes the previous awareness of the essential structure of reality as such.[20]

"The good is that for which all things strive." But what is it that all beings strive for? "All beings strive for their perfection."[21] "The good" is perfection and all that is conducive to it.[22] The concept of perfection, which here, in a sense transcending the ethical, is taken to mean fullness of being (having become filled or complete), includes and comprises these concepts: imperfection, the perfecting process, possibility of being (potency), realization, reality (act), becoming. Therefore, as Saint Thomas expressly states, the word *perfectio,* in the strict sense, cannot be applied to God.[23]

In every reality there is "that" and "what," existence and essence. In God existence and essence are absolutely identical. In a finite creature, however, essence and existence are distinct. The creature "is" its nature only in germ *(in potentia)*. It "becomes" the nature which is to be realized. God alone is absolutely "in being"; the creature, man, is "becoming". "Becoming" is the transition of essence from the state of germinal potency to the state of actuality. At the beginning of every

[19] *ST* I, II, 94, 2.

[20] Here we are not dealing with the question how the reason—considered psychologically—attains the concept of the good; whether it is formed, as Cathrein thinks, spontaneously from the natural inclination of the subject. Nor are we concerned with the problem whether the objective presuppositions which are included in the concept of the good are fulfilled consciously and actually and controllably in the intellect.

[21] Omnia appetunt suam perfectionem. *ST* I, 5, 1.

[22] But goodness signifies perfection which is desirable and consequently of ultimate perfection. Hence, that which has ultimate perfection is said to be simply good. *ST* I, 5, 1 ad 1. Good has not only the character of the perfect but also that of the perfective. *Ver.* 21, 3 ad 2.

[23] Perfectionis nomen, si stricte accipiatur, in Deo non potest poni, quia nihil est perfectum nisi quod est factum. *Ver.* 2, 3 ad 13.

becoming there is a minimally realized essence; at its end (perhaps unattainable) there is a maximal, realized, completely
perfected essence. The "formula" of this movement is: the real
becomes what it is.

But the good is nothing else than this goal and end of the
movement of being, the realization of the essence. "Everything has as much of goodness as it has of being."[24] Perfection
and the good mean nothing else than the "plenitude of being",
plenitudo essendi.[25] The source which feeds the movement of
anything real is the natural inclination of every being to become what it is.[26] And because the good, in this sense, has the
character of a goal and end, "it happens that the reason naturally seizes as a good everything toward which man has a natural inclination."[27] The good, then, is that toward which the
real naturally moves, but this is its own realization. The good
is the real fulfilled in being; the good is the real at the goal of
its movement.

Hence, the voice of the primordial conscience says: the real
should move toward that toward which it tends by its nature
to move.[28] This expresses, first of all, a total affirmation of the
meaning of the world. Secondly, the voice of the primordial
conscience, as the basic first principle of human action, indicates the ethical necessity of man's conscious self-coordination
with the direction of the movement of total reality.

This meaning of the primordial conscience and its voice become clearer if we consider the natural law, which, as we have
already said, is immediately related to the primordial con-

---

[24] Unumquodque tantum habet de bono quantum habet de esse. *ST* I, II,
18, 1.

[25] The good or evil of an action, as of other things, depends on its fullness
of being or its lack of that fullness. *ST* I, II, 18, 2.

[26] *ST* I, 48, 1.

[27] Quia vero bonum habet rationem finis, malum autem rationem con-
trarii, inde est quod omnia illa, ad quae homo habet naturalem inclinationem,
ratio naturaliter apprehendit ut bona et per consequens ut opere prosequenda,
et contraria eorum ut mala et vitanda. *ST* I, II, 94, 2.

[28] We may recall here the passage quoted under 10.

science. "The natural law is nothing else than the participation of the rational creature in the eternal law."[29]

"The eternal law is the voice of divine wisdom which moves all things toward the proper end."[30] Saint Thomas understands the concept of law somewhat differently than our present usage. We think of "law" as the objective command, which, after it has been expressed, has a kind of independent existence between the lawgiver and the people. Saint Thomas sees in the law above all the *act* of commanding, as it is really existent in the mind of the lawgiver: *in principe existens.*[31] The eternal law, as the divine command addressed to the whole of reality, is so effective that every natural inclination in creatures is nothing else than its expression bearing witness to and affirming itself. This divine command is so intrinsic to reality that it is actually identical with the interior operation of the nature of things. If we take the eternal law, in the sense in which the concept of law is at present generally understood, as the objective command of the lawgiver, which has, so to speak, taken up its own position, then we can define it as the inherent directive of total reality itself, which has received and continues to receive its impulse from the wisdom of God.

And the natural law "not different from the eternal law"[32] is nothing else than this very inherent directive of all reality insofar as it is recognized and affirmed by man, who, through his reason, participates in the eternal law. The natural law demands of rational creatures first of all the affirmation, the imitative carrying out, and the preservation of the natural order of the world.[33] Secondly and essentially, it demands that man

[29] Lex naturalis nihil aliud est quam participatio legis aeternae in rationali creatura. *ST* I, II, 91, 2.

[30] Lex aeterna nihil aliud est quam ratio divinae sapientiae, secundum quod est directiva omnium actuum et motionum. *ST* I, II, 93, 1.

[31] *ST* I, II, 91, 1.

[32] . . . if the natural law were something different from the eternal law; whereas it is nothing but a participation thereof. *ST* I, II, 91, 2 ad 1.

[33] Cf. J. Mausbach, *Katholische Moraltheologie* (Münster, 1918–22), vol. 1, 55.

must place himself under the obligation of the sentence, "Become what you are," a statement in which the inherent direction of all reality is expressed. It is reason, the basis and the means of that "participation in the eternal law",[34] which reveals to man his own inherent direction toward self-realization. Through his rational knowledge man can take the law of his being, which inheres in him, and make it his own commanding voice; whereas irrational creatures follow the law of their being only passively. It is not present within them as their own act. Upon this recognition of the natural inclination of being all virtue depends. "The virtues make us able to follow in the proper manner our natural inclinations which belong to the natural law."[35]

Much more could be said about the concepts of the eternal and the natural laws, on which the whole ethics of Saint Thomas and of classical theology is built. But even these brief remarks have probably revealed something of the secret bond connecting the primordial conscience with objective reality.

The voice of the primordial conscience, which is the basic principle of all human action, is determined by being, which presents itself to cognition. The determination is as follows: the knowledge—connected with reality—of the basic structure of all beings and, above all, of man himself—in other words, the knowledge of the urge toward self-realization, born of the tension between existence and essence, which are not identical—is transformed into the command of the primordial conscience. The natural basic structure of reality, above all of man himself, is, in the voice of the primordial conscience, turned to the will. It is knowledge become command, and it carries with it an obligation. The fundamental essential structural "law" of reality, by means of natural knowledge, becomes, in the voice of the primordial conscience, the basic *moral* law of all human action.

[34] *ST* I, II, 91, 2.
[35] Virtutes perficiunt nos ad prosequendum debito modo inclinationes naturales, quae pertinent ad ius naturale. *ST* II, II, 108, 2.

Chapter Eight

Prudence

The voice of the primordial conscience is always "right". Consideration, judgment and command can be right or wrong, true or false.[1] The right consideration, the right judgment and—above all—the right concrete command, these are the acts of the virtue of prudence. The primordial conscience is the naturally and necessarily correct disposition of the practical reason, insofar as it passes judgment about the end and goal of human action. Prudence is the proper disposition of the practical reason insofar as it knows what is to be done concretely in the matter of ways and means. Prudence is not guaranteed by natural necessity as the primordial conscience is; it is the fruit of fallible knowledge and of the free decision of the will.

Prudence is, as Saint Thomas says, partly cognitive *(cognoscitiva)* and partly commanding *(praeceptiva)*.[2] The commanding quality of prudence, into which "consideration" and "judgment" flow, is the expression of its relation to concrete willing and acting; the cognitive quality is the expression of its determination by the objective world of being.

The dependence of willing and acting upon prudence lies in this: the command of prudence is the "measure" of the concrete moral action of the will.[3]

Cf. for this whole section J. Pieper, *Traktat über die Klugheit.*

[1] "Psychological" and "moral" considerations of the primordial conscience therefore coincide. Hence, there can be no objection to including the act of the primordial conscience in the "processus psychologique de l'acte humain". Cf. the review of the first two editions of this book by Odon Lottin, *Recherches de Théologie ancienne et médiévale* I, 61 and 4, 543.

[2] . . . prudentiam, secundum id quod est cognoscitiva, . . . secundum quod est praeceptiva. *ST* II, II, 48.

[3] The truth of practical intellectual virtue . . . in relation to the appetite has the character of a rule and measure. *ST* I, II, 64, 3.

It may at first seem surprising that here the same concept of measure appears which we found in the relation of reality to our knowledge. At least one might have some doubt whether "measure" here meant exactly the same as it does there. But at any rate Saint Thomas undeniably understood the term "measure" in the same sense in regard to the dependence of willing and working upon the command of prudence and in regard to the formation of knowledge by reality. He expressly compares, under the aspect of "measure", the relation of reality and knowledge and the relation of the practical reason to concrete moral action.[4] Both relations are symbolized by the image of the relation of the artist and his work.[5] Furthermore, the causality of the measure is presented to us as the "exterior formal cause", and Saint Thomas attributes this same formal causality to the command of prudence in its relation to the whole sphere of moral actions and virtues.[6] Finally, to describe the relation of prudence to moral action, Saint Thomas uses the words "identity" and "conformity", which are also used to describe the relation of knowledge to reality.[7]

In the command of prudence the morally good action is "pre-formed." Through it the action is "what" it is. The command of prudence therefore is—as measure, that is, as the "exterior essential form"—the model of the moral action. The concrete moral action is essentially an imitation; it has a constitutive relation to something prior by nature. This something prior by nature to all moral action is the command of

[4] Ad ea, circa quae ratio operatur, se habet ut regula et mensura; ad ea vero, quae speculatur, se habet ratio sicut mensuratum et regulatum ad regulam et mensuram. *Virt. comm.* 13.

[5] Idem ergo est medium prudentiae et virtutis moralis; sed prudentiae est sicut imprimentis, virtutis moralis sicut impressi; sicut eadem est rectitudo artis ut rectificantis et artificiati ut rectificati. *Virt. comm.* 13.

[6] All the other moral virtues . . . are formed through prudence as by a proximate form. *Ver.* 14, 5 ad 11. Prudence supplies the form in all other moral virtues. *ST* 3, d. 27, 2, 4, 3.

[7] The rectitude of reason is the mean of moral virtue and also the mean of prudence—of prudence as ruling and measuring, of moral virtue as ruled and measured by that mean. *ST* I, II, 64, 3. Cf. also the sentence quoted under 6.

prudence. The moral action is not "of itself" good, but it is good because it receives its measure from prudence. The morally good and prudence are—as that which receives the measure and that which provides the measure—identical in their "what". They differ only in their place in the order of realization. The good is the imitation (after form) of the prudent; the prudent is the original form of the good. The morally good action is the command of prudence, transformed into a new mode of existence.

Prudence as knowledge receives the measure, and prudence as command provides the measure. The command of prudence is, as Saint Thomas says, a "directing knowledge", *cognitio dirigens*.[8] A commentator on the *Summa Theologica,* the Cardinal Thomas de Vio (Cajetan), speaks of an "active knowing".[9]

The proper and characteristic quality of prudence is the concrete command directed toward willing and acting, but this command is the transformation of previous knowledge. Prudence is the measure of morality, but it first receives its measure from the objective reality of things: "The virtue of the practical reason receives its measure from reality."[10]

And this reception of the measure consists in knowledge being formed by reality. Of this we have spoken enough. "In the *same* way the 'proper mean' in the virtues of the theoretic reason and in those of the practical reason is determined by their conformity to reality."[11] The command of prudence is preceded by its theoretic perceptive identity with objective being.

The question arises upon what areas of reality "prudence as knowledge" turns to receive its measure. "Prudence applies a

[8] *Virt. card.* 1.

[9] Notitia activa, qualis convenit prudentiae. Caiet. in *ST* I, II, 57, 4.

[10] Verum autem virtutis intellectualis practicae, comparatum quidem ad rem, habet rationem mensurati. *ST* I, II, 64, 3.

[11] Eodem modo accipitur medium per conformitatem ad rem in virtutibus intellectualibus practicis sicut in speculativis. *ST* I, II, 64, 3.

general knowledge to particular circumstances."[12] "Therefore it is necessary that the prudent person should know the general basic principles of reason as well as the individual facts with which moral action deals."[13]

The "general basic principles of reason" denotes above all the voice of the primordial conscience, which influences all subsequent partial acts of the whole moral action. The previous voice of the primordial conscience actually makes prudence possible. It works immediately in and with the command of prudence, though not as the most proper and essential element of prudence itself.

Thus, the area of being which belongs properly to "prudence as knowledge" consists of the particular realities and circumstances which "surround" every individual moral action. It is, in a word, the concrete situation of the concrete action, the knowledge of which — besides the natural awareness of the voice of the primordial conscience — is the prerequisite of the command of prudence.

In the command of prudence the knowledge of the concrete situation becomes "directive"; the situation itself, transformed into knowledge and command, turns to the will and imposes an obligation.

[12] Prudentia applicat universalem cognitionem ad particularia. *ST* II, II, 49, 1 ad 1.

[13] To prudence belongs not only the consideration of the reason but also the application to action, which is the end of the practical reason. But no man can conveniently apply one thing to another unless he knows both the thing to be applied and the thing to which it has to be applied. Now actions are in singular matters; and so it is necessary for the prudent man to know both the universal principles of reason and the singulars about which actions are concerned. *ST* II, II, 47, 3.

Chapter Nine

Digressions

Three digressions may be necessary here as answers to questions which have probably risen in the mind of the reader; thereby the contour line of the real purpose of this book will appear more clearly.

First, some readers perhaps expected that we would deal more explicitly with "conscience", but the doctrine of conscience, insofar as it belongs in the context of this investigation, is found not only in our remarks about the primordial conscience but also in our discussion of prudence. Besides and after the primordial conscience *(synderesis)*, the "situation-conscience" *(conscientia)* takes part in the decisive formation of human actions. But the "situation-conscience" which is not, like the primordial conscience, directed to the highest fundamental principles but to the "application" of these principles, is, when it does not err, prudence itself, insofar as the latter considers, judges and commands rightly.[1]

Therefore, it is not surprising that Saint Thomas in his *Summa Theologica* deals specifically with the "situation-conscience" *(conscientia)* in only one article,[2] but with prudence in ten "questions" (fifty-six articles).[3] Moreover, in the reversal of this situation by the newer "Thomistic" moral systems, which hardly speak of prudence but much more of the subjective conscience, we may rightly see a departure from the actual ontological foundation of the ethics of Saint Thomas.[4]

---

[1] "La conscience droite et certaine n'est autre qu'un acte de la prudence, qui conseille, qui juge pratiquement et qui commande." Garrigou-Lagrange, *Du caractère métaphysique de la théologie morale de St. Thomas, en particulier dans ses rapports avec la prudence et la conscience. Revue thomiste,* 8. Cf. also B. H. Merkelbach, *Summa theologiae moralis* (Paris, 1932), vol. 2, 42.

[2] *ST* I, 79, 13.

[3] *ST* II, II, 47–56.

[4] This reproach is expressed, e.g., quite plainly by Garrigou-Lagrange in the article referred to under 1.

Secondly, the question of moral obligation and its basis, which is usually bound up with the doctrine of conscience, lies outside the context of this investigation. The basic question of this study of reality and the good concerns the derivation of the "what" of moral commandments from our knowledge of objective reality; the other question concerns not the "what" but the "that", the obligatory quality of the moral imperative. There it is a question of the relation of dependence between the commanding lawgiver and the one commanded; here the question concerns the content and structure of the commandments and their determination by reality.

We do not deny that the superiority of being also affects the question of moral obligation. An absolute and unconditional obligation is only the echo and reflection of an absolute dependence of being. We can speak of unconditional obligation only in the relation of an absolutely independent and an absolutely dependent being; that is, in the relation of God and the creature.

Out of this idea there grows—thirdly—as it were spontaneously, the thought, which must be taken very seriously, whether the reference to the name of God should not have been made more emphatically than we seem to have made it.[5]

In philosophical ethics God may be considered from two points of view: first, as the supreme lawgiver upon whose absoluteness the unconditional nature of moral obligation is based. We have already remarked that, and in what way, this problem lies outside the compass of our present work. Secondly, God may be considered in philosophical ethics as the creator of man and of the whole finite reality which is related to our knowing and willing as immediately authoritative. Reality has received its measure from God. It is itself the immediate measure of our knowing and willing.

There is a sentence of Saint Thomas in which he, perhaps surprisingly, defends himself against the charge of an ethical

[5] Cf. the review of the first edition of this book in *Divus Thomas* (Freiburg, Switzerland) 9, 100ff.

"short cut" to the absolute. In the *Quaestio disputata* about the cardinal virtues, one "objection" is as follows: the definition of virtue as being according to reason is improper, because reason in turn is subordinate to a higher norm, God himself. Therefore, we must say that the nature of virtue is in this, that it is according to God. To this Saint Thomas replies: "The virtues are subordinated to the reason as their nearest or immediate norm, but to God as their ultimate norm. But objects are specified according to their specific and nearest principles, not according to their ultimate principles."[6] Thus, our study of the good as that which is "according to reality" need not press on to the last and absolute norm, provided only that finite reality is not taken to be this absolute norm.

The "positive", revealed, divine law is something different. Its content is immediately fixed by God himself. But in this supernatural sphere the statements of philosophical ethics, if they are true in themselves, remain in force. They are presupposed and receive a new and more valid guarantee. Moreover, in the sphere of the supernatural in which faith receives the "measure" of a new being, which could not be experienced otherwise, it still holds true that the good is that which is according to reality. It is good for man to live and act according to the measure of the reality revealed by God.

---

[6] Virtutes morales attingunt rationem sicut regulam proximam, Deum autem sicut regulam primam. Res autem specificantur secundum propria et proxima principia, non secundum principia prima. *Virt. card.* 1 ad 10.

Chapter Ten

Objectivity as an Ethical Attitude

The moral action of man, then, is bound up with reality, with "objects", in this way: the concrete act of the will can be retranslated into the preceding "command" of the practical reason. In their "what" they are identical. The "command" of the practical reason can be retranslated into knowledge. It is nothing but transformed knowledge. Moral action is "doing the truth", *veritatem agere*. The knowledge of the theoretical reason is in the identity of its "what" with the objective world of being, with the "things" from which it receives its "measure". This is an unbroken chain of providing and receiving the measure. Knowledge is reality become subjective, the "command" is directive knowledge, and moral action is a command that has become real.

Objectivity, as the right attitude in knowing, is the fitting answer to the fact that knowledge is essentially determined by reality. Objectivity as an attitude in knowing means that the subject, as subject, refrains from taking any part in determining the content of knowledge. This attitude on the part of man guarantees true knowledge.

In the ethical sphere "objectivity" means that the attitude of refraining is also extended to all subjective influencing of the "command" and of the action itself, whose content must be determined only by the objective knowledge of reality if a man's action shall be called "good". It is not necessary to say how much, for instance, the realization of justice among mankind, the supreme and fundamental moral virtue, is directly bound up with "objectivity".

If objectivity in knowledge means recognizing the fact that the content of all knowledge is determined by objects, then in ethics it means further the recognition of the fact that both the interior "command" and the outward action are determined by knowledge. It means that "the attitude of the subject is dictated by the objective *logos,* by the spirit and the *ratio* of the object which he is confronting."[1]

The nature of the practical reason lies in this, that it—first of all in the act of prudence, which is, so to speak, the same thing as "objectivity"[2]—carries out human action by transforming true knowledge into prudent "commands" and prudent "commands" into good actions in relation to the objective reality of "things". To be the passageway for these "things" is the purpose of knowledge and of the "command".

But it would be a mistake to think that by such considerations we would eliminate the subject as subject or degrade it to a mere passageway for objective processes. Cognition, the command, and the exterior action are not "processes" or "occurrences", but acts and deeds of the subject. Without the spontaneous power of the mind and without the impetus of the driving will, none of these acts would ever come to pass. Bringing knowledge, "command" and exterior action into existence, transforming knowledge into "command" and "command" into action—all this is the essentially subjective and basically incomprehensible accomplishment of man, rooted in his personal character and expressing his position in the hierarchy of being, qualitatively superior to all "things".

The thesis that reality is the measure of the good in no way touches or disputes either the originality and individuality of the will or the spontaneity of the subject.[3] Moreover, "objectivity" in knowing is not the same thing as passivity, as we have already stated, and, as an ethical attitude, it is not the same as neutrality, lack of emotion, coldness, indifference.

[1] D. v. Hildebrand, *Die neue Sachlichkeit und das katholische Ethos.* Der Katholische Gedanke 4 (1931).

[2] The concept of prudence emphasizes more the relation to willing and action; the concept of objectivity stresses more the relation to reality.

[3] Cf. the reviews of the first editions of this book in the *Revue Bénédictine,* 44, 84ff.; in the *Revue des sciences philosophiques et theologiques,* 19, 718ff. and 20, 791ff.; in the *Bulletin Thomiste* 9, 529ff.; in the *International Journal of Ethics,* 42.

"Objectivity" and passion may well be combined. The demand for objectivity which we have here—following the "universal teacher" of the Church—derived from the metaphysical nature of human knowledge and action, is found in manifold form in the treasury of wisdom of the human race.

In the book *Tao-te-king* of Lao-tse we read the truly classical sentence: "He who regards himself does not shine" and again: "To act and take no account of it—that is profound virtue."[4] The sentence of Saint Bernard of Clairvaux, which was quoted on the first page of this book, may have been almost a commonplace during the Middle Ages. Three centuries after Bernard, Thomas à Kempis incorporated it almost verbatim into his *Imitation of Christ*.[5] When people no longer understood the word play (*sapiens* = wise, from *sapere* = to taste) which underlies the sentence, its content and meaning also seem to have been lost to view. The deep feeling for reality in the mature Goethe rediscovered this meaning. Many of his statements have been incorporated in this book. We shall quote one sentence from his conversations with Eckermann, which deserves special consideration in our voluntaristic times: "Every epoch which is in the process of retrogression and disintegration is subjective, but all progressive epochs have an objective trend."[6]

The idealist ethics of the last century has largely forgotten and denied the determination of morality by reality. But "ethical realism" receives very significant corroboration from the fact that modern psychology, beginning from an entirely different starting point, and influenced especially by the discoveries of psychiatry, emphatically declares that "objectivity" is one of the most important prerequisites of psychic health.[7] And we cannot value too highly the significance of this fact:

[4] Chap. 24 and 51. In the translation of Viktor von Strauss and Torney.
[5] Bk. 2, chap. 1, 31.
[6] Jan. 29, 1826.
[7] Cf. J. Pieper, *Sachlichkeit und Klugheit. Über das Verhältnis von moderner Charakterologie und thomistischer Ethik*. Der Katholische Gedanke 5 (1932).

that the inherent therapeutic wisdom of natural psychic and mental life itself reveals the same condition as the basis of health which the ethical and metaphysical consideration of the nature of the created spirit recognizes as the basis of holiness.

Chapter Eleven

Summary

The central concept of the classical Christian theory of moral action is the concept of the practical reason. This concept mirrors the dependence of moral conduct upon reason and also the dependence of reason upon reality, and thereby the dependence of moral conduct upon reality. In the unity of practical reason and theoretic reason, epistemological realism is united with ethical intellectualism to form an "ethical realism". This twofold relation of the practical reason—to the world of being and to willing and action—represents the metaphysical, ontological basis of classical Christian ethics.

We shall summarize the result of the preceding study in three statements: the first starts from the concept of the practical reason in general, the second from the practical reason as primordial conscience, the third from the practical reason as prudence.

The practical reason is the measure and the formal cause of morality. At the same time it is essentially one with the theoretic reason, and so is reality of being become the subject. *The measure and formal cause of morality is reality of being become the subject.*

The voice of the primordial conscience is the chief guiding principle and the natural presupposition of morality. It is the practical fundamental principle. At the same time it is the essential structural law of reality, and especially of man himself, which has become directive knowledge. *Therefore, the chief guiding principle and natural presupposition of morality is the basic law of reality and especially of man himself, which has become directive knowledge.*

The command of prudence is the immediate measure and formal cause of concrete moral action. At the same time it is the concrete situation of concrete action become directive knowledge. *The immediate measure and formal cause of concrete moral action, therefore, is the concrete situation of concrete action become directive knowledge.*

CONCLUSION

In the second part of the *Summa Theologica*, in a *question* about the "proper mean", we find an objection which could very easily be passed over but which is the occasion for a statement in which the whole question of *Reality and the Good* is answered succinctly but completely. The objection is as follows: "If the 'proper mean' of moral virtue is determined by intellectual virtue, that is, by prudence, then the proper mean of prudence would, in turn, have to be determined by another virtue, and so we would have an infinite series." Saint Thomas replies: "It is not necessary to proceed to infinity in the series of virtues, for the measure and norm of intellectual virtue is not some other virtue, but the thing itself *(ipsa res)*."[1]

Prudence is the measure of the good, but the measure of prudence is not something within the subject, nor yet immediately "God in the conscience", but reality. Prudence determines what is good, but what is prudent is determined by "the thing itself".

Reality, received in knowledge, is not only the first thing given, from which the free will of man begins to move outward toward the world; it is also the final criterion within the world, justifying in retrospect this outward movement.

---

[1] Non est necesse in infinitum procedere in virtutibus; quia mensura et regula intellectualis virtutis non est aliquod aliud genus virtutis, sed ipsa res. *ST* I, II, 64, 3 ad 2.

THE STRUCTURE OF MORAL ACTS

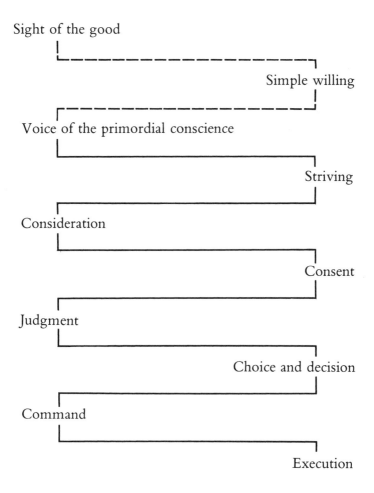

Sight of the good

Simple willing

Voice of the primordial conscience

Striving

Consideration

Consent

Judgment

Choice and decision

Command

Execution

[The left side of this diagram shows the succession of the cognitive partial acts, the right side that of the volitional.]

APPENDIX

SOURCES

This book is based upon a revision of the author's work *Die Wirklichkeit und das Gute nach Thomas von Aquin* (Münster, 1931 and 1934), which in turn presented a different treatment of an earlier work, *Die ontische Grundlage des Sittlichen nach Thomas von Aquin* (Münster, 1929).

In the footnotes the quotations from the *Summa Theologica* of Saint Aquinas are marked by numbers (e.g., *ST* II, II, 47, 2 ad 3 refers to the second part of the second section, question 47, article 2, reply to the 3rd objection); the same thing holds true for the questions from his commentary on the *Sententiae* of Peter Lombard (e.g., *Sen.* I, d.19, 5, 1 equals Book I, distinction 19, question 5, article 1). The titles of the other words are — with the usual abbreviations — as follows: *Summa contra Gentiles (CG), Quaestiones disputatae de veritate (Ver.), Quaestiones disputatae de malo (Mal.), Quaestio disputata de virtutibus in communi (Virt. comm.), Quaestio disputata de virtutibus cardinalibus (Virt. Card.), Quaestiones disputatae de potentia Dei (Pot.), De natura verbi intellectus (Nat. verb. int.), Quaestiones quodlibetales (Quol.), Expositio super S. Pauli epistolam ad Romanos (Rom.), Expositio super S. Pauli epistolam ad Colossenses (Col.).*

The statement of Saint Bernard of Clairvaux which is prefixed as a motto is found in his *Sermones de diversis* 18, 1; Migne, *Patrologia Latina*, vol. 183, 587. The sentence of Goethe is taken from his "Maximen und Reflexionen", no. 530 (edition of Günther Müller, *Kröners Taschenausgabe*).

ABBREVIATIONS

Source references are generally given in short form, with full information supplied in the bibliography. Sources given without the author's name are works by Thomas Aquinas. The following abbreviations are used:

An.	*Quaestio disputata de anima*
Caus.	*Super librum de causis expositio*
CG	*Summa contra Gentiles*
Col.	*Expositio S Pauli epistolam ad Colossenses*
Joh.	*Expositio in evangelium Joannis*
Mai.	*Quaestiones disputatae de malo*
Met.	*In duodecim libros metaphysicorum expositio*
Nat. verb. int.	*De natura verbi intellectus*
Periherm.	*In libros peri hermeneias expositio*
Pot.	*Quaestiones disputatae de potentia Dei*
Quol.	*Quaestiones quodlibetales*
Rom.	*Expositio S. Pauli epistolam ad Romanos*
Sen.	*Sentences*
Sent.	*Scripta super libros Sententiarum*
ST	*Summa theologica*
Symb.	*Expositio super symbolum Apostolicum*
Trin.	*Expositio super librum Boethii de Trinitate*
Ver.	*Quaestiones disputatae de veritate*
Virt. Card.	*Quaestio disputata de virtutibus cardinalibus*
Virt. comm.	*Quaestio disputata de virtutibus in communi*

INDEX

A

Albertus Magnus, Saint,
  on Augustine, 67
  and Leibniz, 18
  teachings of, 20–22
  on transcendental truth,
    15, 69
Alexander of Hales, 66–67,
  76, 99
André, Hans, 99
Anselm of Canterbury, 65,
  99
Aristotle, 14
  on body and soul, 94
  commentaries on,
    65–66, 69
  and the concept of
    truth, 70–71, 79
  on ethics, 97
  on the human soul,
    84–85
  on reality, 129
  on transcendental truth,
    15, 29
  on truth and intelligibil-
    ity, 56, 57
  and truth as knowabil-
    ity, 60
Augustine, Saint,
  and anthropology, 88
  and the concept of
    truth, 65–70, 76, 79
  on God's artistry, 44–46
  on reality, 113

  on transcendental truth,
    29
  and truth as knowabil-
    ity, 61
Averroes, 65–70, 99
Avicenna, 65–66, 76, 99

B

Bacon, Francis, 15–16, 99
Baeumker, Clemens, 31,
  99
Baumgarten, Alexander
  Gottlieb, 99
  on the concept of truth,
    75
  lectures on metaphysics
    by, 36
  and structured reason,
    24–25
  teachings of, 21–23
Bernard of Clairvaux,
  Saint, 108, 173, 179
Bernhart, Joseph, 142
Bochenski, J. M., 31, 99
Bonaventure, Saint, 18, 46
Buchner, Paul, 88

C

Cajetan, 165
Carboni, 28
Cathrein, Victor, 159
Clasen, Carl T., 99
Clauberg, Johann, 75
Cramer, Daniel, 75

Haneberg, B., 101
Hartmann, Nicolai, 101
Hegel, Georg Wilhelm
    Friedrich, 24–25
Henricus (Henry of
    Ghent), 74
Herder, Johann Gottfried
    von, 47–49, 101
Hervaeus, 74
Hettner, Hermann, 47, 101
Hilary, Saint, 61, 112–113
Hildebrand, 171–172
Hildebrandt, Kurt, 25, 47,
    85, 102
Hobbes, Thomas, 16, 102
Hoffman, Nicolai, 60–63
Horten, Max, 66
Hufnagel, Alfons, 27, 36,
    102

I
Iamblichus, 14

J
Jacobi, Friedrich Heinrich,
    47–49
Jansen, Bernhard, 17, 102
John, Saint (the apostle),
    41, 45–46, 58

K
Kant, Immanuel, 102
    on the concept of truth,
        76
    on God's artistry, 67
    precritical period of, 23

and Spinozism, 47–49
and structured reason,
    25
on theoretical and prac-
    tical reason, 142–143
on transcendental truth,
    19–21
Keckermann, Bartholo-
    mäus, 74–75
Klasmeier, Wilhelm, 71,
    102
Kluge, Friedrich, 30
Knittermeyer, Hinrich, 102
    on Albertus Magnus, 15
    on Augustine, 67
    on Keckermann, 75
    on metaphysical truth,
        21
    on Thomas Aquinas, 32
Knutzen, Martin, 21
Kremer, R., 26–27, 60,
    102
Kriszat, G., 105
Kroner, Richard, 142
Kühle, Heinrich, 69, 102

L
Lao-tse, 173
Lasswitz, Kurd, 16, 102
Leibniz, Gottfried Wilhelm
    von, 102
    teachings of, 20–21
    and truth as knowabil-
        ity, 60
    and universal harmony,
        18